THE CHURCHES THE APOSTLES LEFT BEHIND

THE BEST-KNOWN APOSTLES (Peter, Paul, James) all died in the decade of the 60s. Thus, in the last one-third of the first Christian century, the early churches had to go on without the authoritative guidance of the apostles who had seen the risen Jesus. The New Testament works written after the death of the apostles illustrate different emphases that enabled the respective communities addressed by those works to survive. Studied here are both the strengths and weaknesses in the ecclesiologies of seven different New Testament witnesses. These witnesses are addressed to the churches the apostles left behind, but their strengths and weaknesses speak to the churches today.

THE CHURCHES
THE APOSTLES LEFT BEHIND

Raymond E. Brown, S.S.

PAULIST PRESS
New York/Ramsey

Cover and jacket design by Jon Bauch.

*Cover and jacket drawing
by Mother Maria of the Holy Spirit, O.C.D.*

Nihil Obstat:
Myles M. Bourke, S.S.L., S.T.D.
Censor Deputatus

Imprimatur:
Joseph T. O'Keefe, D.D.
Administrator, Archdiocese of New York

Date:
January 17, 1984

Library of Congress Cataloging-in-Publication Data

Brown, Raymond Edward.
    The churches the apostles left behind / Raymond E. Brown.
    —New York: Paulist Press, c1984.

    156 p.; 21 cm.

    Bibliography: p. 151-152
    Includes indexes.
    ISBN 0-8091-2611-7 (pbk.): $5.95. — ISBN 0-8091-0352-4 (hard)

    1. Church history—Primitive and early church, ca. 30-600.   2. Apostles.   3. Bible. N.T.—Criticism, interpretation, etc.   I. Title.

BR165.B698   1984   270.1—dc19   83-82159
                        AACR 2   MARC

Published by Paulist Press
997 Macarthur Blvd.
Mahwah, N.J. 07430

Printed and bound in the
United States of America

This book, which I think of as ecumenical, is dedicated to biblical scholars from Christian backgrounds other than my own who, through their studies and especially through personal friendship, have taught me much about the Scriptures, about Christ and about his Church, and most of all about being a Christian. I think in particular of the following on the American scene with an awareness that the list is far from complete:

Paul Achtemeier
Karl Donfried
Reginald Fuller
J. Louis Martyn
D. Moody Smith

Edward Campbell
John Elliott
Beverly Gaventa
John Reumann
Krister Stendahl

W. D. Davies
David Noel Freedman
George Landes
James Sanders
Phyllis Trible

PREFACE

THE CONTENTS OF THIS BOOK were given as the Sprunt Lectures at Union Theological Seminary (Richmond, Virginia) in five sessions on January 28–31, 1980. Care in the choice of Sprunt lecturers, plus the obligation to publish, has produced a notable series of lecture volumes. While flattered to be invited to join such a company, I faced immediately a problem arising from the very history of the series. The obligation to publish and the past quality of publications suggested an erudite contribution to scholarship; but the needs of the audience, who consisted of Union alumni working in churches, suggested a practical application of scholarship to pastoral interests. Explicitly choosing to meet the latter need in my lectures, I did not write out and read papers filled with scholarly footnotes; rather I spoke from notes, orally adapting as I went to the responses of the audience that sat before me. This accounts partially for a delay of several years in the publication of the lectures; for I had to put them in written style, working on the tapes and notes of what I said in 1980. Greater detail, documentation, and updating have been added to the published form which, I hope, while preserving the original pastoral intent, will meet the demands of scholarship inherent in the "Sprunts."

The interlude between presentation and publication proved a happy development, for I was able to represent the same material to other audiences and thus to grow in my perception of the issues. For that reason I would like to acknowledge gratefully the opportunity of having offered forms of the material now printed in various chapters of this book in the Cole Lectures at Vanderbilt Divinity School

(Nashville, Tenn.), in the Ayer Lectures at Colgate Rochester Seminary (New York), in the Snuggs Lectures at the University of Tulsa (Oklahoma), in the Rist Lectures at Iliff School of Theology (Denver, Colorado), in the Armstrong Lectures at Kalamazoo College (Michigan), and in the Weber Lectures at the Moravian Theological Seminary (Bethlehem, Pa.). The ecumenical aspect of my approach to the subject was greatly enhanced by this history of diverse audiences.

I was the first Roman Catholic invited to give the Sprunt Lectures; the Roman Catholic Bishop of Richmond attended the opening lecture; and of great assistance to me during my lecture period at this southern Presbyterian Seminary was their first Roman Catholic doctoral candidate in Biblical Studies. The audience of pastors, solidly Presbyterian in their own formation, must have found in these visible signs an expression of the ecumenical context of theological education and biblical studies in seminaries today. With an attempt at humor, I sought to reassure the audience of my orthodox credentials stemming from the fact that I held a Presbyterian-sponsored Chair at the "other" Union Theological Seminary in New York, where my professorship has been supported partially by Auburn Theological Seminary.

In order to give a foretaste of my intentions in the Sprunt Lectures, I dared to share with the audience a rather funny moment of my existence for a decade as the sole Roman Catholic professor at the northern Union Seminary. When I first came, there was still in the catalogue an introductory claim that the faculty represented "the wide range of theological and church outlook which is characteristic of Protestantism at its best." The anomaly of having this catalogue statement in the light of the presence of a Roman Catholic professor was brought to the President's attention, and he asked me if I found the statement offensive. With tongue in cheek, I replied, "No, for I think that a balanced Roman Catholic represents the *best* in Protestant outlooks." These offhand introductory remarks underlined my deliberate intention in Richmond to speak from the New Testament to the various church situations that exist today. Questions asked me at the Sprunt Lectures enriched the presentations in this volume by enabling me to anticipate issues that might arise in the minds of many readers. The task of rephrasing the material in lectures at other

Protestant seminaries, as indicated in the history above, has facilitated my goal by making me more conscious of an even wider Christian diversity. It has also been helpful that I have used this material with many Roman Catholic audiences and tested their reactions.

My last three books were dedicated to Roman Catholic bishops and clergy who have given valued support to modern Catholic scholarship in general, and to my own in particular. Now this volume of lectures given at a Presbyterian seminary might, I thought, be dedicated appropriately to Protestant scholar friends to whom I am indebted in many ways. Outside scholarship, despite ecumenical advances, there are Protestant clergy who still distrust anything said by a Roman Catholic. The warmth of the reception given me by the alumni of Union Seminary in Richmond encouraged my thinking that a negative reaction is not characteristic of good Protestant pastoral care. I know also that there are many Roman Catholics who distrust everything Protestant and are infuriated by a Roman Catholic acknowledging a debt to Protestants. When Pope Paul VI appointed me to the Roman Pontifical Biblical Commission, he graciously commended my "Catholic regard for the Magisterium of the Church." Loyalty to one's own church and an indebtedness to a wider scholarship are a combination that has enriched my appreciation of what New Testament diversity can mean to various churches—a combination that I would defend against all criticism.

I intend this volume to be a companion to two other books that I have written in recent years. *The Community of the Beloved Disciple* was an attempt to study the history of one group in New Testament (henceforth, NT) times—the Johannine community with its peculiar internal and external life story. The volume I did with John P. Meier, *Antioch and Rome,* was an attempt to study two great Christian NT centers. Here I am investigating Christian communities from the viewpoint of their diverse understanding of what was important for survival and growth after the death of the apostles. All three books represent different approaches to church existence in the NT period. All three are meant to speak to the churches today by way of corrective, challenge, and encouragement. To my mind such is the task of exegesis: not only to determine what the NT situation was, but also to ask what it means.

I distressed some of my coreligionists in my *Birth of the Messiah* when I stated (p. 9): "I see no reason why a Catholic's understanding of what Matthew and Luke meant in their infancy narratives should be different from a Protestant's." I was accused of denying the Catholic teaching that church tradition interprets Scripture. I was not denying it at all, but normally church tradition has not interpreted what a biblical author *meant;* it has interpreted what his work means to a living community. I am painfully aware that Catholic and Protestants can be at one as to what Scripture meant but divided as to what it means. In this book, however, since our different churches often face the same problems, I am hoping that there will be some meeting of minds as to what NT church strengths and weaknesses can mean to Christians today.

Union Theological Seminary (NYC)
August 15, 1983

TABLE OF CONTENTS

TABLE OF CONTENTS

CHAPTER 1

The Sub-Apostolic Era in the New Testament[1]

IN "A DEATH IN THE DESERT" Robert Browning poetically describes John, the last apostle, expiring in concealment:

> When my ashes scatter, says John, "there is left on earth
> No one alive who knew (consider this!)
> —Saw with his eyes and handled with his hands
> That which was from the first, the Word of Life.
> How will it be when none more saith, 'I saw'?"

Browning's fidelity to the tradition that John was the last of the apostles may have been too simple, but his poignant question is perceptive. How was it when the last apostolic witness disappeared from the scene, and the church could no longer depend on the testimony of those who said, "I saw"? In the past that question was answered by turning to works written after the NT because it was assumed that the NT and the apostolic era were coterminous. NT books were thought to have been written by apostles, and the era after the NT was dubbed "sub-apostolic." In Catholic tradition this view was

---

1. Because, as explained in the Preface, this book is a practical application of scholarship to pastoral interests, citations in the footnotes favor English works. Complete information is given in the footnote unless the book appears in the bibliography. In the latter case, the author's last name and a word or two from the title are supplied in the footnote.

summed up in an axiom about revelation closing with the death of
the last apostle, which assumed that the NT lay safely within the apostolic lifetime.[2] Today, however, most scholars would date the end
of the apostolic period earlier and thus within the NT era. Indeed, if
one does not accept Bishop John A.T. Robinson's maverick attempt[3]
to date the whole NT before A.D. 70, it can be claimed intelligently
that *most of the NT was written after the death of the last* known
apostle.

Perhaps that qualified statement needs to be explained. Although many are called "apostles" in the NT, we have detailed
knowledge of only three. If we begin with the Twelve, most are no
more than names. If one excludes Judas Iscariot, the first four alone
stand out, namely, the two sets of brothers: Peter and Andrew,
James and John. Although in the gospels those four are portrayed as
frequently in the company of Jesus, in the NT story of the early
church Andrew disappears; James is martyred in the early 40s (Acts
12:2); and John is mentioned only as a shadow companion of Peter in
a few scenes (3:1; 4:13; 8:14; Gal 2:9). Later tradition enhanced the
biography of John by identifying him as the Beloved Disciple of the
Fourth Gospel tradition, but that is far from certain.[4] In fact, then,
Peter is the only member of the Twelve of whose ecclesiastical career
we are substantially informed, thanks to the Pauline Letters to Galatia and Corinth, the Book of Acts, and to epistles in the Petrine tradition. Outside the Twelve we know a great deal about *Paul* the

---

2. That axiom continues to be valid against those who would promote new
bodies of revelation binding upon all Christians. The axiom means that God's *ultimate*
self-revelation was in His Son Jesus—He can give us no more of Himself—and that
the essential Spirit-guided witness to this revelation was in and through the apostles, a
witness enshrined in the NT. The axiom does not mean that the apostles completely
understood the revelation, for the understanding of divine revelation is an ongoing
process.

3. Among the many critical reviews of his *Redating the New Testament* (London: SCM, 1976), helpfully incisive is that by J.V.M. Sturdy, *Journal of Theological
Studies* 30 (1979) 255–62: "an ultimately unconvincing *tour de force.*" Robinson "one-
sidedly ignores difficulties for his views, steamrollers the evidence, again and again advances from an improbable possibility into a certainty."

4. The distinguished Roman Catholic scholar, Rudolf Schnackenburg, in the
final volume of a study that took ten years, *The Gospel according to St John* (3 vols.;
New York: Crossroad, 1968–82) 3.375–88, came to the conclusion that the Beloved
Disciple (who was not the evangelist but the authority behind the Gospel) was not one
of the Twelve. See also my *Community* 33–34.

Apostle, thanks to 13 letters attributed to his name in the NT and to biographical information supplied by the Book of Acts. *James,* "the brother of the Lord," was probably an apostle, even though not one of the Twelve. His importance as leader of the Jerusalem community[5] is attested both in the Pauline Letters and the Book of Acts; also a NT letter is attributed to him, and the letter of Jude identifies its author through relationship to James. According to reasonably reliable tradition, Peter and Paul died in Rome in the 60s, and James died in Jerusalem in the 60s.[6] Thus, by the end of the second third of the century, i.e., by the year A.D. 67, the three apostles about whom we have detailed NT knowledge had disappeared from the scene.

I suggest, therefore, that the term "Apostolic Age" should be confined to that second one-third of the first century, and that *the last one-third of the century should be designated as the "Sub-Apostolic Period."* With the exception of the undisputed letters of Paul,[7] most of the NT would have been written in this last one-third of the century—a period when the authors who are preserved in the NT wrote without using their own names and occasionally under the mantle of the apostolic forebears. (An exception would be the otherwise unknown prophet named John who identifies himself as the author of the Apocalypse or Revelation.) Later tradition tended to assign authors to the originally anonymous gospels;[8] but modern scholarship has called into doubt the accuracy of those assignments which, in any case, may have been meant to tell us more about the authority behind the individual work than about the actual writer.

---

5. The dispute as to whether he was the son of Mary and Joseph, or a more distant relative of Jesus (the son of Joseph by a previous marriage, or a cousin, etc.) need not conern us here. His importance was not due to his following Jesus during the ministry, but to his family relationship, plus his being accorded a vision of the risen Jesus (I Cor 15:7).

6. For a brief survey of the evidence, see Barrett, "Pauline Controversies" 233–35.

7. There is overwhelming agreement that Paul himself composed I Thessalonians, Galatians, I and II Corinthians, Romans, Philippians, and Philemon. That list reflects the order of composition I think probable; I suggest a date in the 50s for the first four, leaving open a possible date in the early 60s for the last two. The attribution of other NT letters to Paul is disputed by scholars (see the beginning of Chapter 3 below). I refer to those as Deutero-Pauline epistles.

8. No evangelist identifies himself by personal name; titles such as "The Gospel according to _____" are a late second-century addition.

As for the Deutero-Pauline epistles (the Pastorals, Ephesians and Colossians[9]) and the Catholic epistles, the designation of the authors as Paul, James, Peter, John, and Jude probably represents a claim to apostolic adherence rather than an objective designation of apostolic writing. Indeed, a namelessness of the actual writers fits in with a sub-apostolic ambience where fidelity to the memory of the great apostles is the dominant characteristic.

In the terminology that I favor, the "Post-Apostolic Period" begins at the end of the century when we have Christian writings put forth on their own authority, e.g., the Letters of Ignatius of Antioch and the Letter from the Church of Rome to the Church of Corinth known to us as *I Clement.* This written work of a "third generation" was moving away from claiming the direct mantle of the apostles.[10]

Returning, then, to Browning's poem, I would move his scene of the death of the last apostle back to the mid-60s—a date that makes no less important the question of how was it "when none more saith, 'I saw.' " Now, however, we can use most of the NT to answer that question.

VARIOUS SCHOLARLY APPROACHES
TO THE SUB-APOSTOLIC PERIOD

In the past and reaching up into the present there have been many attempts to answer the question that Browning phrased poetically. If in the following brief summary I indicate the inadequacies of some of them, ultimately it will be seen that each has a grain of truth. No one view is totally adequate, and the deficiencies in some of the proposals I shall mention warn us against hoping that the answer can be simple.

The classical answer, already given in *I Clement* (42 and 44), is

---

9. Many scholars would include II Thessalonians; but since I shall not treat that work in detail in this book, this debated point need not be discussed.

10. The language of "three generations" for the Apostolic, Sub-Apostolic, and Post-Apostolic Periods is a convenient generalization, so long as it is not taken too literally. Nor are all writings covered by my distinction that second-generation NT works are written in the name of (or under the mantle of) apostles, while third-generation works often are not. II Peter belongs to the third or fourth generation and yet claims the mantle of Peter, and apocryphal works of the second and third centuries bear apostolic names.

that just as Jesus appointed apostles (understood to be the Twelve along with Paul), so also the apostles appointed bishops or presbyters to succeed them. Consequently, there was understood to have been an orderly succession of authority in the sub-apostolic era producing a unified church, marred only by heretics who were seen as rebels against the stipulated system.[11] That classical thesis began to be rejected at the time of the Reformation and has been effectively challenged by modern scholarship (both Roman Catholic and Protestant) which has shown that the Clementine picture was too simple and not universal.[12]

In the last century another answer was given by F. C. Baur whose thesis, at least for a while, also became classical. In Baur's somewhat Hegelian conception of church history, the thesis and antithesis were represented by James (or even Peter) and Paul—a pro-Jewish conception of Christianity in struggle with a pro-Gentile one. A period in the second century saw the synthesis of what preceded, and the image of Peter was invoked to symbolize a Christianity intermediary between that of Paul and of James. Integral to the Baur hypothesis was a very late dating of some documents used to substantiate the sequence, e.g., Acts. Much of modern scholarship would challenge such dating and would consider the various Christian attitudes detected by Baur to have been simultaneous and quite early.

In the 20th century other answers to the question of sub-apostolic Christianity have been offered. Walter Bauer[13] argued that NT Christianity and its immediate sequence constituted an era in which there was no standard or orthodox Christianity. Rather from many early diverse and contending Christian views there emerged in the second century a victor which became orthodoxy; this orthodoxy moved from Rome eastwards. Most scholars would acknowledge

---

11. Later church writers like Hegesippus (Eusebius, *History* 3.32.7; 4.22.4) would picture the church of the first century as a virgin, pure and "not yet corrupted by vain teachings." S. Cohen, *Union Seminary Quarterly Review* 36 (1980–81) 1–11, compares rabbinic and Christian views on the origins of respective heresies and finds them remarkably alike.

12. See, for instance, the chapter on the episcopate in my *Critical Meaning* 124–46.

13. W. Bauer, *Orthodoxy and Heresy in Earliest Christianity* (Philadelphia: Fortress, 1971; Germ. orig. 1934).

some of the diversities Bauer posited in the NT period; but recently
there has been an increasing chorus of objections[14] that Bauer's hypothesis is too simplified and leaves unanswered fundamental questions. For instance, was what emerged from the diversities by
"winning out" more faithful to what Jesus of Nazareth taught and
represented than were the Christian views that lost the struggle?[15]
From reading Bauer and his proponents, one can easily get the impression that all diversities were of equal value and that what
emerged as orthodoxy was simply a historical accident, or the survival of the strongest rather than survival of the fittest.

Another modern answer was that of Kirsopp Lake[16] who interpreted the Sub-Apostolic Period in terms of great Christian city-cen-
ters. In Jesus' lifetime his ministry had fluctuated between Galilee
and Jerusalem. In the Apostolic Period, if we confine our attention
to the West, centers like Jerusalem, Antioch, and Corinth flourished.
In the late Apostolic and Sub-Apostolic Periods, according to Lake,
Ephesus and Rome emerged as the great Christian centers with
which many NT books can be associated. Rome was deemed to represent Jewish Christianity, more conservative from the very start,
and a proponent of a high ecclesiology and a low christology.[17] Relat-

---

14. See the excellent summary of reactions by D. J. Harrington, *Harvard Theological Review* 73 (1980) 289–98; reprinted in *Light* 162–73. Called into question are
Bauer's late dating for the emergence of orthodoxy and his claims that this orthodoxy
was imposed by Rome, and that the first Christianity in Egypt and Syria was heretical
(by the standards of later orthodoxy). A better diagnosis of diversity is given by
J.D.G. Dunn, *Unity and Diversity in the New Testament* (Philadelphia: Westminster,
1977).

15. See D. J. Hawkin in *Eglise et Théologie* 7 (1976) 367–78. Why is it not possible to see the "orthodoxy" that emerged as exhibiting both theological balance and
historical balance (G. R. Flora, cited by Harrington, 295), and to see it as "crystalliz-
ing self-awareness" rather than as an accident of power (R. A. Markus, *New Black-
friars* 54 [1973] 283–84)? R. H. Fuller, "New Testament Trajectories and Biblical
Authority," *Studia Evangelica VII* (Berlin: Akademie, 1982) 189–99, suggests that orthodoxy may be viewed not as static but as directional, so that the orthodox church
fathers would have followed a trajectory leading from the Christ event. See ftnote 201
below.

16. Lake, *Landmarks*, esp. 75–103.

17. High christology means a presentation of Jesus that places greater emphasis
on his divinity and association with God; low christology places greater emphasis on
the human career of Jesus (without necessarily denying or omitting his divinity).

ed to Rome, in Lake's judgment, were Paul's Epistle to the Romans, I Peter, the Epistle to the Hebrews, *I Clement,* and the *Shepherd of Hermas.* (In fact, however, there are many elements of high christology in Hebrews; and in my judgment, it can be associated with Rome only as a corrective sent to modify Rome's Judaizing tendencies.) Related to Ephesus were Colossians, Ephesians, and the Fourth Gospel—works with a low ecclesiology, in the sense of placing little emphasis on church structure, but with a high christology which associated Christ with creation. Recent scholarship might find confining Lake's concentration on two Christian centers, for certainly Antioch[18] and Alexandria were also in the picture in the sub-apostolic and/or post-apostolic eras. Nevertheless, his detection of a Christianity that was more conservative and more closely associated with Judaism (Rome) and of a Christianity that was more volatile (Ephesus) remains a valid insight.

In this book I shall proceed in a manner different from the approaches discussed above, even though there is some truth in each which may complement my approach. *I shall examine a number of different church situations reflected in the sub-apostolic works of the NT* (i.e., the works written in the last one-third of the first century), *concentrating on the most important element that enabled each church to survive after the apostolic hero or guide had departed the scene.*

DIFFERENT CHURCHES DETECTABLE IN THE NEW TESTAMENT

Before the chapters devoted in detail to individual churches, it might be well in this introductory chapter to survey the communities or churches detectable in the sub-apostolic NT works. (The number would be even larger if one made use of second-century material, including gnostic writings, and retrojected the situations reflected in those works back into the first century; but the scope of the lectures reproduced in this book dictates that I confine myself to the NT.) In subsequent chapters I shall not discuss in detail all the communities

---

18. Meier, *Antioch* 12–86.

that I now list, but it may be helpful to the reader to have the general survey.[19]

Let us begin with the sub-apostolic descent of *Paul.* Despite the powerful personal impact of the apostle on those whom he converted, an intelligent case can be made that within 20 years after his death variant strains of thought had developed within the communities influenced by Paul. In a fascinating article C. K. Barrett[20] has shown that at least three different post-Pauline strains can be detected through an analysis of NT works associated with Paul: one exemplified by *the Pastoral Epistles,* one exemplified by *Colossians and Ephesians,*[21] and one exemplified by *Luke/Acts.* I plan to dedicate a chapter of this book to each of these strains; but even now, it may be wise to illustrate diversity among them.

Although the audiences or communities respectively addressed by these works all knew of Paul, it is not certain where the audiences were located geographically[22] or whether they knew each other. The author of Luke/Acts idealizes Paul, for he divides Christian history into almost equal eras centered on Peter and Paul. The latter embodies God's plan to move Christianity from Jerusalem to Rome and to "the ends of the earth." Yet the author of Acts never mentions that Paul wrote a letter and betrays no knowledge of the Pauline letters. In the strain of Pauline heritage represented by Colossians and Ephesians Paul is greatly honored as the apostle who can authoritatively address the communities—indeed as one of the apostles (and proph-

---

19. If the reader is unfamiliar with modern scholarship about how and when NT books were written, helpful on a beginning level is Pheme Perkins, *Reading the New Testament: An Introduction* (New York: Paulist, 1978). For detailed, technical argumentation, see W. G. Kümmel, *Introduction to the New Testament* (rev. ed.; Nashville: Abingdon, 1975).

20. Barrett, "Acts"; also his "Pauline Controversies." See de Boer, "Images of Paul," and Conzelmann, "Die Schule."

21. Barrett speaks of Ephesians, not of Colossians. Very probably the author of Ephesians did not write Colossians; but he used it as his chief source, and *in relation to the question I shall ask below* the two letters are close enough in thought pattern to reflect a similar strain.

22. The destination of Colossians to Colossae in Asia Minor is relatively undisputed. Whether Ephesians really was sent to Ephesus is textually uncertain since "at Ephesus" in 1:1 is missing from the best Greek manuscripts. Apparently the Pastorals are addressed to Timothy in Ephesus and to Titus on Crete, but it is impossible to determine how much of the setting of the Pastorals is fictional. Nothing in terms of place is known of the community or groups who were addressed in Luke/Acts.

ets) upon whom the church is founded (Eph 2:20). It is also very clear that the author of Ephesians knew many of the Pauline letters, even beyond Colossians, and that he draws upon them in formulating his own thought. Thus, while both the author of Luke/Acts and the author of Ephesians have moved beyond Paul's thought, one has done so seemingly independently of Paul's writings, and the other has done so in marked dependence on them. Are we not to think this difference was manifest also in the image of Paul possessed by the communities formed by these authors?

Let us consider another issue, namely, the relation to Judaism. In Ephesians the relationship between Jew and Gentile seems to have been solved pacifically. The wall of hostility has been broken down; those who were once far off have come near; Jew and Gentile are reconciled in one body to God through the cross (Eph 2:11–22). For the author of Acts (28:25–29), however, the very last words of Paul terminating the book indicate the Jews will never see, nor hear, nor understand; they are permanently closed off from the gospel. Salvation, according to the Paul of Acts, is for the Gentiles who will listen and understand. In other words, in the different communities addressed by these works—communities that both respect Paul—there may have been very different views about the future relations of Jews and Gentiles. Both attitudes are at a distance from that of the historical Paul in Romans who argues that the Gentiles were converted to make the Jews jealous, that ultimately the Jews themselves will be converted, and that the Gentiles are but a wild olive branch grafted onto the tree of Israel (Rom 11:11–26).

When we turn to the Pastoral Epistles, namely to I and II Timothy and Titus, we find still a different post-Pauline situation. The author of these works remains troubled by Judaizers (among others) and their demand for circumcision. In Chapter 2 below I shall discuss in detail the strong insistence of the author of the Pastoral Epistles on church structure and the appointment of church officials. This is an insistence that is lacking in both Colossians/Ephesians and Luke/Acts, even though both works know of church functionaries. We shall see below that the author of the Pastorals, the author(s) of Colossians/Ephesians, and the author of Luke/Acts have a very different dynamism in what they emphasize as important in their respective conceptions of the church. All this variation occurs within the Pauline tradition in works that are directly or indirectly related to the apostle! Presumably, the churches addressed by such works, if they were in contact, would have been in *koinōnia* or communion with each other—at least there is nothing explicit in the works to indicate otherwise—but their ways of thinking are different because they have emphasized different aspects of the great Pauline tradition.

If such variations exist within the one heritage, not surprisingly there are variations among different heritages in the Sub-Apostolic Period. In a recent book, *The Community of the Beloved Disciple,* I have studied **the Johannine community** (or communities,[23] since by the time of I John there had been a secession). One might find some similarity between the Fourth Gospel and Colossians/Ephesians in terms of a high christology in which the pre-existent divinity of Jesus is underlined. Such a christological criterion, however, would distinguish Luke/Acts from the Fourth Gospel (and from Colossians/Ephesians) since there is no explicitation of pre-existence in the Lucan writings. In terms of relation to Judaism, the Fourth Gospel would differ markedly from all three Pauline strains discussed above. In John the Christians have been driven out of the synagogues (9:22; 16:2); the Jews are virtually another religion—or are worse, since they have the devil as their father (8:44). The liturgical feasts inherited from the OT are now feasts "of the Jews" (6:4; 7:2) and, therefore, do not pertain to Christians. Indeed, Jesus is scarcely thought of as a Jew and can speak of the Jewish law as "their law" (15:25). Even if tradition has placed the writing of the Fourth Gospel in Ephesus, the same city addressed (in some manuscripts) by the Epistle to the Ephesians, one can scarcely imagine that in Johannine Christianity the wall of hostility between Jew and Gentile has been broken down, as in the situation envisaged by Ephesians.

I mentioned above that Kirsopp Lake identified Ephesus as one of the two great Christian centers of the Sub-Apostolic Period, a center with a distinctive theology. More likely, Ephesus had different

---

23. It may be debated whether, in a book on the sub-apostolic churches of the NT, one should discuss the secessionists of I John 2:19, since the epistolary author regards them as denying Christ (2:22). Surely, however, this group, although dubbed "secessionists," regarded themselves as the true heirs of the Johannine Gospel. For them the epistolary author and his followers would have been the secessionists. See Brown, *Epistles* 69–71.

churches with different theologies.[24] We must remember that the Christian situation in a large city would have involved a number of house churches where 20 or 30 people met together; and so there is no reason why there could not have been in the one city house churches of different traditions—for example, of the Pauline tradition, of the Johannine tradition, of the Petrine or apostolic tradition, and even of the ultraconservative Jewish-Christian tradition. Even though the house churches of one tradition probably had *koinōnia* with those of another tradition, Christians may not have transferred easily. Furthermore, in II and III John it is clear that, once an inner Johannine secession had taken place, within the same tradition[25] there was no longer *koinōnia* between the two sides, or admittance to the respective house churches (II John 10; III John 9–10).

Related directly to the Ephesus area and related indirectly to the Johannine Community of the Fourth Gospel and the Epistles[26] would have been the recipients addressed in the **Book of Revelation.** The bitter remarks about the "synagogue of Satan" and "the Jews" (Rev 2:9; 3:9) suggest once again a group in which the wall of hostility had not been broken down (unlike Eph 2:11–22). Revelation has affinities to the Fourth Gospel in the theme of replacing Jerusalem and the earthly Temple by a heavenly Jerusalem and the presence of God and Christ. Nevertheless, the apocalyptic insistence on final eschatology is so unlike the stress on realized eschatology in the Fourth Gospel that one has strong reason to doubt that the two works were addressed to the same recipients at the same time.[27] The Johannine relationship to the recipients of Revelation may have been

---

24. See my "New Testament Background for the Concept of Local Church," *Proceedings of the Catholic Theological Society of America* 36 (1981) 1–14.

25. In the *Epistles* I contend that both the epistolary author and his adversaries accepted Johannine tradition such as that found in the Fourth Gospel, but interpreted it differently. Frequently inner-Christian conflicts occur not because one group accepts a foundational document that the other rejects but because two groups interpret differently a document both accept.

26. For similarities between Revelation and the Johannine writings, see O. Böcher in *L'Apocalypse johannique et l'Apocalyptique dans le Nouveau Testament,* ed. J. Lambrecht (Bibliotheca Ephemeridum Theologicarum Lovaniensium 53; Gembloux: Duculot, 1980) 289–301.

27. Nevertheless, there are strains of final eschatology in the Fourth Gospel as well (see my Anchor Bible *John,* 1.cxvi-cxxi), precisely because that Gospel in its final form preserves elements from various stages in Johannine theological history.

at most that of distant cousins. I am tempted by the thesis that those addressed in Revelation were heirs of the Johannine tradition who (perhaps because of early migration from Palestine or of early missionary activity to Asia Minor) had not been catechized by the fourth evangelist,[28] or by his companions, and so were *not* affected by the major theological synthesis of Johannine tradition known to us in the Fourth Gospel.

This early departure from the Johannine stream could explain some affinities of thought between the seer of Revelation and the writer of the Johannine Epistles, since the latter deliberately went back to "the beginning" of the Johannine Gospel tradition (I John 3:11) to refute those who were distorting the Fourth Gospel by interpreting it independently of earlier presuppositions.[29] Both Revelation and I John stress the sanctifying cleansing power of Christ's blood (Rev 1:5; 5:9; 7:14; I John 1:7 and 5:6–8). Both works stress final eschatology much more than does the Gospel. Nevertheless there are differences. The epistolary author by implication knows of false teachers (I John 2:27) and false prophets (4:1) among those who seceded from the Johannine Community, but among his own followers he rejects human functionaries like teachers (and probably prophets) in favor of the Gospel tradition of the Paraclete-Spirit who will teach all things and will announce the things to come (John 14:26; 16:13). For Revelation, however, there are prophets in the communities (Rev 11:10; 16:6);[30] indeed the author himself (1:3; 22:9,19) is a prophet. Revelation knows also of false prophets (16:13) and of false teachers who seemingly have not yet been expelled from the community (2:20). Neither the Fourth Gospel nor the Johannine epistles speak of the apostles, while Revelation shows respect for "apostles and prophets" (18:20) and special veneration for *the* Twelve Apostles of the Lamb (21:14). Such a reference to twelve as the number of the apostles implicitly challenges Paul's insistence that he was an apos-

---

28. See the treatment of Johannine dating in my *Community,* 96–97; I attribute the evangelist's writing of the Fourth Gospel to *ca.* A.D. 90. The Johannine Epistles may have been written a decade later. I date Revelation within that decade of the 90s.

29. See *Epistles* 97–100.

30. Elisabeth Schüssler Fiorenza treats Revelation in the context of early Christian prophecy in *L'Apocalypse* (ftnote 26 above) 105–28. She dissociates Revelation sharply from the Johannine writings.

tle. Another difference from Paul would be reflected in the anti-imperial attitude of Revelation: the Roman Empire and emperor worship are the beastly puppets of Satan (chap. 13) and the numerical value of Nero's name (666) is the number of the beast (13:18). Certainly this differs from the pro-imperial attitude attested in Rom 13:1–7 (and in other works associated with Rome in the last 40 years of the first century, such as I Pet 2:13–17; *I Clem* 60:4–61:1).[31] These collective observations are meant to show that while Revelation has affinities with the Johannine heritage, and even the Pauline heritage, it cannot be easily classified in either camp.

Similarly, the outlook expressed by the author of **Hebrews** has certain Johannine and Pauline parallels but remains quite distinct. (Hebrews is a corrective writing, but here I am concerned with the Christian outlook that Hebrews supports rather than the one that it corrects.[32]) As for a Johannine relationship, Hebrews is close to the Fourth Gospel in proclaiming Jesus as God, a Son through whom the world was created (Heb 1:2–3,8).[33] Nevertheless, John does not attribute to Jesus' humanity the limitations that one finds in Hebrews, e.g., being tempted (4:15), learning obedience (5:8), and being made perfect (5:9). Certainly the Johannine Jesus who refused to pray to be delivered from the hour of death (John 12:27–28) could not be described as crying out with tears to God who was able to save him from death (Heb 5:7). As for a Pauline relationship, in the Eastern churches and later in the universal church Hebrews was thought to constitute the fourteenth letter of Paul—a view virtually no scholar holds today. The style of Hebrews is totally different from Paul's, and there is nothing in the Apostle's writing to match the prolonged radical critique of Israelite cult that is at the heart of Hebrews. Indeed in Romans chaps. 9–11 and 15:16, Paul shows himself far more preservative of Judaism and its cultic language than does Hebrews which would replace the OT sacrifices, priesthood, and Tabernacle.

---

31. Brown, *Antioch* 137–38, 172–73, 180–82.

32. *Ibid.* 139–58: it was meant to *correct* a Roman Christianity that had very strong attachments to Jerusalem and the Jewish cult.

33. The parallels between Hebrews and John are carefully studied by C. Spicq, *L'Epitre aux Hébreux* (2 vols.; Paris: Gabalda, 1952) 1.92–138.

The radical attitude of Hebrews toward Judaism (similar to that of the Fourth Gospel) separates it from the mindset of at least three other sub-apostolic works of the NT (I Peter, James, and Matthew). Although **I Peter** is written in the name of the first of the Twelve, it is thought by most scholars to have been written by a Petrine disciple after Peter's death. Elsewhere I have argued that it represents the outlook of the Roman church to which Hebrews was addressed as a corrective.[34] Below I shall devote a chapter to I Peter, and so here let me simply report that 1:13 – 2:10 applies to Gentile converts the whole Exodus experience of Israel, so that *they* have left their former servitude, and been redeemed by the blood of a lamb, while going through a period of wandering toward a promised inheritance. If for Hebrews the levitical priesthood has been replaced by Christ, for I Peter the Christian people constitute a royal priesthood. Preservation and reapplication, rather than replacement, mark the theology of I Peter. The language of Judaism is used as if it belongs to Christianity and there are no other claimants.

Even more Jewish is the outlook of the Epistle of **James.** If I Peter is addressed to the chosen exiles of the diaspora (plausibly Gentile Christians), James is addressed to the twelve tribes in the diaspora (perhaps Jewish Christians). James 2:2 assumes that the Christian addressees are assembling in a synagogue. There are no passages dealing with christology, but there is an insistence on the morality of the prophets of Israel: Religion is "to visit orphans and widows in their affliction" (1:27); and no partiality must be shown to the rich over the poor (2:1–7). It is possible, then, that James is addressed to a Christian community in the last third of the century where belief in Jesus meant a heightening of Jewish values but no real divorce from Judaism. We know that in post-NT literature such as the Pseudo-Clementines James became the hero par excellence of Jewish Christians who did not differ from Jews over the Law but only over faith in Christ. An incipient form of such a development may account for the appeal to James as the authority behind this canonical epistle, for in it we hear: "Whoever keeps the whole Law but fails in one point has become guilty of all of it" (2:10). Certainly the emphasis that "one is justified by works and not by faith alone"

34. Brown, *Antioch* 128–33.

(2:24) reflects values different from those of Paul in Rom 3:28: "One is justified by faith apart from the works of the Law."[35]

Close in many ways to James is the Gospel of **Matthew,**[36] even though it is clear that Matthew is written to a Jewish Christian community that had Gentile Christian adherents in large numbers. This mixed community is taught that not the smallest letter of the Law or a curlicue of a letter of the Law is to pass away until all is accomplished (Matt 5:18). Even though in the attitude of Jesus, "You have heard it said . . . but I say to you" (Matt 5), some very non-legalistic attitudes are inculcated, the perspective is one not of abolishing the Law but of fulfilling the divine purpose behind it. Paul and Matthew might have reached similar practical conclusions about individual obligations, but Paul would have done so on the principle that Christ is the end of the Law (Rom 10:4), while Matthew would have seen Jesus as the perfect and demanding lawgiver of the eschatological period.

A Roman Catholic who praises a non-Pauline stance in the NT is always suspect, but some communities (like that of Matthew) probably did not go through the Pauline crisis about the Law and preserved a more moderate and positive attitude toward the Jewish heritage.[37] If one cannot put new wine into old wineskins without destroying them, Matthew encourages an arrangement that allows the preservation of all the wineskins, both new and old (9:17). The Matthean community's relation to Judaism (see ftnote 183 below) may have been less ruptured than that of the Johannine community, but more troubled than that of the community addressed by James. In a later chapter I shall discuss Matthean ecclesiology after the death of the apostles, an ecclesiology that has had enormous influence in the history of Christianity. For later Christianity Matthew's Gospel was *first,* not simply in the order of the canon.

---

35. The closeness of wording between the two statements and the common appeal to Abraham (with different interpretations of his sanctity) suggest that the author of James had heard a form of Paul's teaching and that he disagreed with the way some appealed to it as a dispensation from doing good works.

36. See M. H. Shepherd, "The Epistle of James and the Gospel of Matthew," *Journal of Biblical Literature* 75 (1956) 40–51.

37. Meier, *Antioch* 62–63, gives a nuanced evaluation of the differences between Matthew and Paul.

I have left to last the community addressed by **Mark**. In a book devoted to "The Variety and Unity of the Apostolic Witness to Christ," L. Goppelt concluded that redaction-historical studies in recent years had not been certain enough to enable him to reconstruct the theological profile of the oldest evangelist.[38] I would be even more certain that such studies do not allow us to reconstruct the profile of the community addressed by Mark (even to the elementary point of being sure whether Mark was reinforcing that community in beliefs it already held or was inculcating beliefs that were absent). For instance, Norman Perrin and a number of younger scholars whose works he endorsed (T. Weeden, W. Kelber, etc.) have argued that an important element in the Marcan community admired the apostles (like Peter) as wonder-workers and as spokesmen of a triumphalistic faith based on the resurrection appearance of Jesus. To correct that admiration Mark wrote a Gospel highly critical of the apostles (especially Peter) as figures who never understood Jesus and never believed—a Gospel where resurrection appearances have been suppressed in favor of a parousia in Galilee. I happen to agree with E. Best[39] and others that this is a wrong reading of the evangelist's intentions. True, Mark describes the Twelve as misunderstanding because Jesus had not yet suffered, but this treatment implies no more then that their important role after the crucifixion required a difficult initiation period—all Christians believe through the prism of the cross, even the greatest. This encouragement is addressed to Christians who are themselves suffering. (If Mark was written to the Roman church,[40] Mark may have wished to reassure the readers that Peter's own recent suffering and death under Nero was not a defeat but a step toward victory.) Mark 16:7 is a reference to a well-known resurrection appearance to Peter, so that in my judgment the parousia in Galilee is a fiction of the interpreter's imagination. Part of the methodological problem is that, while we may be able to diagnose something of Matthew's and Luke's theology by seeing how they

---

38. L. Goppelt, *Theology of the New Testament* (2 vols.; Grand Rapids: Eerdmans, 1982) 2.xi (J. Roloff's Foreword).

39. E. Best, *Following Jesus, Discipleship in the Gospel of Mark* (JSNT Supp. Series 4; Sheffield: JSOT Press, 1981).

40. See Brown, *Antioch* 191–201.

change a source known to us (Mark),[41] we do not have Mark's sources. Theories based on the changes Mark made in hypothetically reconstructed sources are too uncertain to be of much use. If one is content to deal with Mark as it now stands, one can get some agreement about what Mark is saying, but not necessarily about why he is saying it. Yet the "why" question is all important for interpreting the outlook of the recipients.

*   *   *

Even leaving aside Mark, we have found a remarkable sub-apostolic variety of thought: witnesses to three different forms of post-Pauline thought (Pastorals, Colossians/Ephesians, Luke/Acts), evidence of two different forms of post-Johannine thought (the epistolary author's adherents and their secessionist adversaries), works with both Pauline and Johannine similarities (Revelation, Hebrews), a post-Petrine witness (I Peter[42]), and some witnesses of a more conservative Christianity respectful of the Law (Matthew, James). I have pointed out significant differences among these witnesses, and their interrelationship is highly complicated. For instance, Luke is related to Pauline thought, while Matthew is quite distinct from Paul; yet the two Gospels share many common features (infancy narratives, virginal conception, use of Q).

As we seek to employ these witnesses to reconstruct *community situations* in the Sub-Apostolic Period, a serious methodological problem is to ascertain whether the thought expressed is peculiar to the author or is truly shared by a community. When one is dealing with epistles or letters, the situation is often easier to determine. Nevertheless, since all of the works have been preserved (and even accepted as canonical), we are certain that at least some Christians found guidance in them. Another methodological problem involves caution about the *partial* extent to which the writing portrays community views. If the Pastorals stress presbyteral structure and Colos-

---

41. That Matthew and Luke depended on Mark is itself a hypothesis, but one that is accorded about 90% agreement among scholars. Reconstruction of Marcan sources is much more problematic.

42. II Peter could also be mentioned. Presupposing I Peter, it is written in the name of Peter; it pays uneasy respect to Paul, while recognizing the distortion of Paul by Pauline enthusiasts (3:15–16); implicitly it draws upon Jude, the brother of James.

sians/Ephesians stress the body of Christ, that does not mean that
the Christians who received the Pastorals and the author who wrote
them were ignorant of the theology of the body of Christ, nor that
those involved in Colossians/Ephesians were ignorant of the presbyteral structure. One can be certain only of the positive emphasis that
Christians were hearing in a particular work.

I hope to avoid some pitfalls by working with that *positive emphasis applied as an answer to a specific question.*[43] In the chapters
that follow I plan to discuss seven sub-apostolic NT witnesses (Pastorals, Colossians/Ephesians, Luke/Acts, I Peter, John, the Johannine Epistles, and Matthew). I wish to see how the different
emphasis in each of these seven witnesses would answer *the question
of survival* after the death of the great first generation of apostolic
guides or heroes.[44] A sociological observation, already made by Max
Weber, is that the problem of continuance and succession is inevitably raised with the disappearance of the original leaders of a movement. The crisis is accentuated to the degree that those leaders have
innovatively moved their followers away from the previous criteria of
authority. By the time of the death of the apostles, the churches were
already breaking away or broken away from much of what previously constituted authority in Judaism; but then (as ever since) they
have had to survive without the living tutorship of the great figures
of the first generation. The answers of their immediate successors
were, I suggest, repeated throughout the ages—not in the sense that
one church repeated one answer and another church repeated another answer, but in the sense that each church has repeated many of
the answers. A difference among modern churches lies in the propor-
tionate arrangement of answers.

---

43. H. Boers, "Contemporary Significance of the New Testament," *Journal of
the American Academy of Religion* 45 (Supp. March 1977) 1–33, follows Gottfried
Martin in insisting that a system of thought be assessed from the viewpoint of questions to which it is an answer: "One does not have to presuppose that the NT writers
took issue with each other, or even knew of each other. It is sufficient if they were
addressing the same problem" (p. 3).

44. Paul would have had this role for the first three witnesses I have mentioned
in the parenthesis; Peter would have had it for I Peter and Matthew; the Beloved Disciple would have had it for John and the Johannine Epistles. As indicated in ftnote 4
above, it is unlikely that the latter was an "apostle," a term significantly absent from
John and I-II-III John.

CHAPTER 2

The Pauline Heritage in the Pastorals: The Importance of Church Structure

I WISH TO BEGIN my discussion of the churches the apostles left behind with three epistles that in some ways constitute the most formal, *ex professo* treatment of sub-apostolic continuance in the NT. Paul spent much of his Christian life as a missionary, adding constantly to the number of those who had come to believe in Jesus Christ. The setting of the two letters written to Timothy and of the one letter to Titus envisions Paul near death: "the time for my departure has come; I have fought the good fight; I have finished the race" (II Tim 4:6-7).[45] Accordingly, his thoughts turn to the Christians he is leaving behind. How are they to survive, especially since an enormous danger is presented by false teachers who could mislead them (Titus 1:10; I Tim 4:1-2; II Tim 3:6; 4:3)? In other words, Paul's interests are now no longer primarily missionary but pastoral; he is concerned with tending the existing flock. Of course, such an interest is not lacking in his early letters, but appropriately these three letters have been dubbed "Pastoral" par excellence.

---

45. I agree with the vast majority of scholars that Paul is already dead and that, by writing in Paul's name, the unknown author is assuming the mantle of Pauline authority in order to meet post-Pauline problems. But what I write above does not depend for its validity on the authorship question. If post-Pauline, the Pastorals preserve certain strains of genuine Pauline thought. See ftnotes 54, 66, and 73 below.

(Let me add parenthetically that a similar shift is found in the image of Peter in John 21. The Synoptic Gospels remember Peter as the fisherman who was turned into a catcher of men [Luke 5:10]. In the first part of John 21 [1–11] Peter makes a miraculous catch of fish and drags ashore a net bulging with 153 large fish. Then the imagery changes abruptly as Jesus ignores the fish and instructs Peter to feed his lambs or sheep [John 21:15–17]. The imagery of fish is quite appropriate for the missionary activity of bringing people into the Christian community, but does not lend itself to the ongoing care of those who are brought in. The hallowed NT image for that is shepherding a flock—the image from which we get the term "pastoral." Just as Paul the missionary, when pictured as dying, becomes primarily Paul the pastor preserving those whom he has converted, so in John 21 there is a shift of imagery from Peter the fisherman to Peter the shepherd. In the Petrine "pastoral epistle,"[46] Peter gives sheep-tending advice [I Peter 5:1–3].)

The dying Paul's advice on how to survive, given to Timothy and Titus, and through them to Christian communities, is clearly and concisely an answer in terms of structure. Some of the Pauline communities are deficient in that they do not have local authorities, but now that deficiency must be remedied and presbyter-bishops are to be appointed in every town (Titus 1:5,7). The authoritative guidance of these men will preserve the local church communities against disintegration.

Elsewhere I have gone into detail on the complicated question of the designation and function of the church authorities in the Pastorals,[47] so let me here by way of background simply list my conclusions. Although the word *presbyteros* (comparative of *presbys,* "old," meaning "elder" in Greek) refers to age, the custom of seeking advice from the senior men of a community meant that "elder" or "presbyter" came to designate a functionary chosen ideally for wisdom, often elder in age but not necessarily so. Jewish synagogues had

---

46. I Peter was probably written after Peter's death by an author assuming the mantle of Peter's authority. (Any critical introduction to the NT discusses the authorship issue.) See the opening of Chapter 5 below.

47. The evidence is cited in my *Priest and Bishop* (New York: Paulist, 1970) 34–43, 65–72; and *Critical Meaning* 136–44. Virtually nothing is known of what deacons did in NT times and how they differed from presbyters.

groups of elders or presbyters who set synagogue policy. Christian presbyters, however, had a pastoral supervising role that went beyond the Jewish counterparts; and so we find them designated by a second title, *episkopos,* "overseer, supervisor, bishop." The oft-made claim that the *presbyteros* is a role borrowed from Judaism while *episkopos* is a role borrowed from Gentile (pagan) secular and religious administration is oversimplified and ignores the evidence of the Dead Sea Scrolls. In the century and a half before Christianity the Essenes described in the Scrolls had, besides presbyters, functionaries called "overseers" with teaching, admonitory, and administrative roles almost identical to those of the bishops of the Pastorals. The Essene religious overseers were figuratively described as "shepherds," even as were Christian bishops (Acts 20:28–29; I Pet 5:1–3). Thus, I think it plausible that from the synagogue Christians borrowed a pattern of groups of presbyters for each church, while the pastoral-supervisor *(episkopos)* role given to all or many of these presbyters[48] came from the organizational model of close-knit Jewish sectarian groups such as the Dead Sea Essenes. There is nothing in the Pastorals to suggest that presbyter-bishops dealt with the eucharist or baptism.[49] Nor do we know how presbyter-bishops were appointed, although by the time Acts was written (the 80s or 90s) Barnabas and Paul could be pictured as having appointed presbyters in *every* church (14:25). That the picture has been oversimplified is indicated by Titus 1:5 where it is clear that there are towns of the Pauline mission without presbyters. According to *Didache* 15:1 (*ca.*

---

48. In Christian writings somewhat later than A.D. 100, e.g., those of Ignatius of Antioch, the pattern of having only one *episkopos* or bishop presiding over a group of presbyters (and deacons) is attested. The fact that the Pastorals use *presbyteros* in both the plural and the singular but *episkopos* only (twice) in the singular has led some to suppose that the regimen of the single bishop was already in effect when the Pastorals were written (80s?). In Titus 1:5,7, however, the two terms are interchangeable, so that there were plural presbyter-bishops in the church of a given town envisaged in the Pastorals. A remark in I Tim 5:7 suggests that not all the presbyters exercised supervision or taught, and clearly the supervising or bishop function is becoming more esteemed.

49. James 5:14, however, shows the presbyters of the church having a special role in prayer over the sick and in anointing. By the time of Ignatius, presiding at the eucharist and at baptism was confined to the (single) bishop or to his delegated replacement.

100?) Christians were invited to appoint for themselves bishops and deacons.

Such background information about presbyter-bishops may be useful, but it should not distract us from those functions of the presbyter-bishops that make them the Pastorals' answer to how Pauline communities will survive after his death. *First* and foremost in the Pastorals the presbyter-bishops are to be the official teachers of the community, holding to the sound doctrine that they have received from Paul through Titus and Timothy and rejecting any novel or different teaching. They can protect the community from false doctrine because they can silence wrong teachers (Titus 1:9 – 2:1; I Tim 4:1–11; 5:17). *Second,* since the church is "the household of God" (I Tim 3:15: a comparison heightened because the church met in a house), the presbyter-bishops are to be like fathers taking responsibility for a home, administering its goods and providing example and discipline. Stability and close relationship similar to that of a family home will hold the church together against the disintegrating forces that surround or invade it.

The qualities demanded of the presbyter-bishop are institutional virtues such as would be appreciated in a tight organization with a familial tone. He must be blameless, upright, and holy; he must be self-controlled and not arrogant or quick-tempered (Titus 1:7–9). He must be able to manage his own home well and control his children (I Tim 3:4). It is implied that he must be able to manage the budget of his own home; in particular, he must not be a lover of money (I Tim 3:3,5)—character requirements all the more important if, as may well be suspected from Dead Sea Scroll parallels, the presbyter-bishop had to administer the common money of the Christian community. A blotch like drunkenness cannot be tolerated on his moral record (Titus 1:7; I Tim 3:3). Indeed, at times the requirements border on matters of religious respectability: he cannot have been married more than once; he cannot be a recent convert; his children must be Christian (Titus 1:6; I Tim 3:2,6).

These latter requirements reflect the emergence of the church as a society with set standards that it is imposing on its public figures. Jesus during his ministry called prominent followers from various walks of life without any consideration how society might look on fishermen, tax collectors, and a zealot.[50] But Jesus was not structuring a society; he did not live in an organized church; the Twelve were selected not as administrators but as eschatological judges of the renewed Israel (Matt 19:28; Luke 22:30). Once the movement associated with Christ became organized enough to be a society called "church," however, it began to decide that certain standards of religious respectability were very important for the common good. Individuals, however talented, who did not meet those standards would have to be sacrificed. The presbyter, after all, had to serve as a model father of a family. A man converted after his children had grown might be a natural leader; but if he did not meet the qualification of having believing children, he was not to be appointed presbyter-bishop. Sometimes recent converts are insecure or not mature in their Christian judgment; other times they are filled with an extraordinary zeal that might galvanize a community. The Pastoral Epistles would allow no recent convert, talented or not, to function in the presbyteral office—almost an ironic requirement, granted the history of the man who is supposed to be writing the letters. Indeed, Paul might not have been able to meet several requirements the Pastorals would impose on the presbyter-bishops. "Not quick-tempered" (Titus 1:7) would scarcely describe the Paul who called the Galatians "fools" (Gal 3:1). "Dignified" (I Tim 3:2) would not fit the Paul who wished that his circumcising adversaries would slip with the knife and castrate themselves (Gal 5:12) and who could utter such vituperation as "Their God is their belly" (Philip 3:19). Rough vitality and a willingness to fight bare-knuckled for the Gospel were part of what made Paul a great missionary, but such characteristics might have made him a poor residential community supervisor. The Pastorals are listing qualities necessary for someone who would have to get along with a community for a long time; fortunately for all, perhaps, Paul's missionary genius kept him on the move.

Naturally, the writer of the Pastorals hopes that individuals with charismatic gifts will be appointed presbyter-bishops, but he is willing to sacrifice charismatic qualities for more pedestrian qualities

---

50. Luke 6:15 and Acts 1:8 call Simon "the zealot," while Matt 10:3 calls Matthew "the tax collector."

that will facilitate harmony in the Christian community. Such an early imposition of community standards should be remembered when a question arises today about the right of the church to set societal standards for its clergy. For instance, I have heard the right of the church to demand a college-educated clergy challenged on the grounds that Jesus did not demand education for membership in the Twelve. The logic of that type of observation should be rejected because of the dissimilarity of situation. As I indicated above, the Twelve were not residential clergy; and Jesus never lived in a structured church. Similarly to be queried is the idea that the requirements imposed by the Pastorals are eternally valid. Rather, since sometimes the requirements have to do with public respectability, they can and should change in the course of time. The primitive church was prejudiced against the remarriage of widowers (I Tim 5:9,11; I Cor 7:8), allowing it only reluctantly for ordinary people. Consequently, the Pastorals would not tolerate remarried presbyter-bishops (I Tim 3:2; Titus 1:6); they should meet the ideal. Today few Protestant churches would refuse ordination to remarried widowers. On the other hand, an echo of being "the husband of only one wife" is found in many Protestant churches that impose on their clergy the requirement of not being remarried after divorce (even though they allow such remarriage for laity). Roman Catholicism has imposed Paul's personal standard ("It is well for them to remain single as I do": I Cor 7:8) on all its presbyters. One can always query the *wisdom* of individual requirements that different churches have made for their presbyterate, but the right to make such requirements seems to have been supposed from the beginning.

Institutionalization of the Christian movement was an aspect of what scholars call "early Catholicizing." (Early Catholicism is often a pejorative designation to cover the emergence of ecclesiastical features found later in Roman Catholicism and deemed objectionable by the Reformers and their spiritual descendants among contemporary biblical scholars.[51]) While judgment on that term and topic re-

---

51. See my brief discussion in the *Jerome Biblical Commentary*, art. 67, #94–97; and the excellent article by D. Harrington, "The 'Early Catholic' Writings of the New Testament: The Church Adjusting to World History," in *The Word in the World*, ed. R. J. Clifford and G. W. MacRae (F. L. Moriarity Festschrift; Cambridge, Mass.: Weston, 1973) 97–113; reprinted in Harrington, *Light* 61–78.

quire nuance, Gager is certainly correct in pointing out that "a good deal of nonsense has been written about the decline of primitive Christianity into 'early Catholicism.' "[52] Rudolf Bultmann would agree with Sohm that "legal regulation [when seen as constitutive] contradicts the Church's nature."[53] Rather, if the church is a society, regulations, constitutive or otherwise, are an inevitable sociological development that is of the nature of the church.

STRENGTHS AND WEAKNESSES

Having described briefly a principal motif in the Pastoral Epistles, namely the stress on church structure, let me now point out both the strengths and weaknesses of such an emphasis as an answer to church continuance after the death of the apostles (or more precisely, after the death of *the* apostle, Paul). I forewarn readers that a section on strengths and weaknesses will also be part of subsequent chapters dealing with other answers. All answers to a theological problem, of necessity being partial and time-conditioned, involve paying a price. One emphasis, no matter how necessary at a particular time, will inevitably lead to a neglect of truth found in another answer or emphasis. I plan to center on three points in my discussion of the strengths and weaknesses of the Pastorals' structural answer: (1) The idea of preserving an apostolic heritage against radical ideas and teachers; (2) The safe institutional virtues required of pastors; (3) The sharp distinction between those who teach and those who are taught.

First, impressive stability and solid continuity are marks of an institutional structure (presbyter-bishops and deacons) designed to preserve the apostolic heritage. The Pastorals have found a way to highlight the uniqueness of the apostle and at the same time to extend his influence beyond his lifetime. Apostolicity is personified in

52. J. W. Gager, *Kingdom and Community: The Social World of Early Christianity* (Englewood Cliffs, NJ: Prentice-Hall, 1974) 67.

53. R. Bultmann, *Theology of the New Testament* (2 vols.; New York: Scribners, 1951, 1955) 2.97–98.

Paul—no other apostle is mentioned and no other is needed[54]—and
this apostle provides for the aftermath of his departure by passing on
his heritage to the presbyter-bishops under the supervision of Timothy and Titus. Emphatically Paul is a teacher, "a teacher of the nations" (I Tim 2:7; see also II Tim 1:11); and the chief function of his
heirs is to teach "sound doctrine" (Titus 2:1), carrying on the guidance given to his converts by the apostle. The bishop must "hold
firmly to the sure word as it was taught" (Titus 1:9). Timothy, who
had been an observer of how Paul taught (II Tim 3:10), is admon-
ished, "Continue in what you have learned and have firmly believed,
knowing from whom you learned it" (3:14).

The enemy against whom this advice is directed are teachers
who are introducing new ideas, a group described as insubordinate
men, empty talkers, and deceivers.[55] Such people love discussion and
controversies (I Tim 6:4–5; Titus 3:9); and they win an admiring following among hearers with "itching ears" (II Tim 4:3), a group that
might be described less pejoratively as having enquiring minds. The
apostle of the Pastorals would have such purveyors of new and different ideas stopped from teaching (I Tim 1:3): "They must be silenced, for they are upsetting whole households by teaching for
dishonest profit what they have no right to teach" (Titus 1:11). The
faithful are reminded to be submissive to rulers and authorities, both
secular and religious (Titus 3:1). In the Pastorals, then, we have the
ancestor of the theology of a deposit of doctrine, and such ecclesiastical developments as the approval of professors, *imprimaturs*, an index of forbidden books, and supervised church presses—features not
unique to Roman Catholicism by any means, even if the same names
are not used in other churches and the control is not as obvious.

The historical circumstances in which the Pastoral Epistles were
written involved great danger for the form of Christianity that would
ultimately be designated "orthodoxy" (pp. 17–18 above). A follow-

---

54. R. F. Collins, "The Image of Paul in the Pastorals," *Laval Théologique et
Philosophique* 31 (1975) 147–73. In Kertelge, *Paulus* 70–121, 122–45, there are nuanced articles on the Pauline heritage in the Pastorals by G. Lohfink and P. Trummer.
The latter (143) points to the importance of the Pastorals in saving the Pauline corpus
canonically for the church and argues (144) that one should not set up the Pastorals
and the undisputed letters as contradictory.

55. See the various descriptions in I Tim 1:3ff; 4:1ff; 6:20–21; II Tim 2:16–18;
3:1–9; 4:3–4; Titus 1:10–16: 3:9.

ing among Christians was already being won by the propagandists of gnosticism (I Tim 6:20: what is falsely called knowledge [*gnōsis*]).[56] The struggle-to-the-death that would culminate *ca.* 180 in the *Adversus haereses* of Irenaeus had now begun. Already the "Paul" of the Pastorals had divined that the best response to a plethora of views claiming to be revealed and even traditional was a pedigreed tradition, involving a link between the apostolic era and approved church officials. Irenaeus would only be refining the argument when he appealed to a chain of bishops of the great Christian centers in his refutation of gnostic doctrines.[57] I would contend that the underlying maxim, "Hold firmly to the sure word as it was taught" (Titus 1:9), remains an essential weapon in times of major doctrinal crisis. It enabled the Roman Catholic Church to survive the tumultuous days of the Reformation; it enabled Luther's movement to survive an anarchical Protestant left-wing *(Schwärmerei)* spawned by his own protest against Rome; today it should enable the mainline churches to survive biblicist sectarians.[58] True, a stringent control over teaching (and writing) exercised by church authorities runs against a democratic sense of freedom of thought and expression; but in the rare moments when theological freedom threatens to become anarchy, "the church of the living God, the pillar and bulwark of the truth" (I Tim 3:15) has the right not to let itself be destroyed from within.

The great danger with an *exclusive stress* on officially controlled teaching, however, is that, having been introduced at moments of crisis, it becomes a consistent way of life. The Pastoral Epistles, shaped by doctrinal crisis, are often read without context as offering a universal and unconditioned policy. Truly pastoral policy, rather, requires a *relaxation* of such stringent controls when the crisis has

---

56. Actually it is not clear that only one form of heretical thought was the target, since I Tim 1:7 and Titus 1:10 envision Jewish or Jewish-Christian opponents who may not be the same as the gnostics.

57. *Adv. haer.* 3.3.3 begins with the succession of bishops at Rome (which the author of II Tim 4:7 may well envision as the place where Paul would "end the race").

58. To speak of biblicist sectarians in the same sentence as radical movements may seem strange, since often they are looked on as ultraconservative in their bible reading. In my judgment biblical fundamentalism as we know it in the English-speaking world is a recent innovation quite foreign to the great exegetical tradition of the church, which has always allowed (but with different nuances) a non-literal element in the Scriptures. Many sectarians retroject nineteenth-century American individualistic pietism into the biblical period.

passed. For instance, having survived both the Reformation and the Enlightenment through controlled teaching, the Roman Catholic Church showed great wisdom in abolishing some of its negative doctrinal controls as an aftermath of Vatican II.[59]

What type of exaggeration may flow from the failure to see that an *exclusive stress* on appointed teachers is a policy conditioned by dangerous times? The fear of new ideas evident in the Pastorals may become endemic in the structured church. There are times when having "itching ears" in the sense of an inquisitive mind is necessary in order to keep the spirit of Jesus from being suppressed. After all, the Jesus who challenged the religious authorities of his time with the dictum, "Let that person hear who has ears to hear" (Matt 11:15; cf. Mark 8:18), could well be accused of having admired itching ears. At certain times the greatest peril facing a well-ordered institutional church is not the peril of new ideas but the peril of no ideas. The community described in the Pastorals would be perfectly safe if no one thought any other ideas than those handed down. Then, however, it might fall under the condemnation of the gospel parable against the servant who was perfectly happy to hand over what he had received, but was considered by Jesus as wicked and slothful because he had added nothing new to it (Matt 25:24–30).

The idea of entrusted truth (II Tim 1:14), translated into a "deposit of faith," is very useful as a corrective against liberal romantics who think that Christian theology can be *created* anew in each generation. It has severe limitations if it projects the image of a safe deposit box sterilely protecting what was put into it in the first century. Every generation must add to the deposit through its unique experience of Christ in its time. The presbyter-bishops of the church must "hold firmly to the sure word as it was taught" to them (Titus 1:9), and woe to them if part of the deposit of faith is lost in their administration. But also woe to them if they do not encourage constructive

---

59. Since pastoral practice responds to existing situations, the stress on official teaching may change frequently in intensity. In the Roman Catholic Church, less than a decade after Pope Pius X's severe stress on controlled teaching in reaction to the Modernist crisis, Pope Benedict XV rejected overly zealous heresy-hunting, espionage, and denunciation. Two decades after the relaxation associated with Vatican II, Pope John Paul II seems to feel a need for tightening some controls again, especially in practical matters of lifestyle.

insights that augment and nuance the sound doctrine they are obliged to teach. A weakness of the Pastorals is that the latter duty is never mentioned.

Second, a related strength and weakness in the Pastorals is a total orientation toward pastoral qualities in the officials of the structure that is to be erected. Through the safe, institutional virtues demanded of the presbyter-bishops (tantamount to prudence, sobriety, and balance), these writings are meant to insure a benevolent, holy, and efficient administration. The "clergy" appointed by Timothy and Titus should have been good, sound people, easy to get along with as resident pastors; but their job profile is not likely to have brought to leadership dynamic "movers" who would change the world. As I point out above (p. 35), the historical Paul could not easily have met the requirements for the local presbyter-bishop. But then the historical Paul was a missionary and never a lifetime resident in a settled community. He had risky new ideas about Christ as the end of the Law and an untamable restlessness that made him highly successful in opening new frontiers for Christ. Traversing those frontiers, whether geographic or intellectual, required an unconventionality frowned on by the Pastorals. Paradoxically, the leaders of the Jerusalem circumcision party opposed to Paul (whom he undiplomatically called "false brethren" in Gal 2:4) may have exemplified well some of the condemnatory attitudes encouraged by the Pastorals, for undoubtedly they regarded Paul as a dangerous teacher of novelties who should be silenced. After all, in their estimation he did not hold on to the sound doctrine taught by Jesus (in the tradition of Matt 5:18), namely that not the smallest letter, not even the smallest part of a letter, of the Law would pass away.[60]

In other words the pastor and the missionary are different roles that characteristically require different strengths. One may justly observe that making new converts was not the problem faced by the "Paul" of the Pastorals. The fact, however, that the Pastorals were

---

60. The Jerusalem meeting on whether the Gentiles had to be circumcised (i.e., become Jews) in order to become Christians is described in different forms in Acts 15 and Gal 2, but in neither account do those who say circumcision is *un*necessary quote the Jesus of the ministry as supporting their position. One may well suspect that the advocates of circumcision were the ones citing the historical Jesus, insisting that *he* never dispensed with the practice.

shaped by the problem then at hand often has not been recognized, and they have been thought to describe an ideal church order adequate for all times. In fact they make no structural provision for ongoing mission activity; and the thrust toward such highly prudential leaders, holding on to the past, creates an orientation that is not going to favor the innovations necessary for a dynamic mission. That recognition becomes all the more important if the pastoral care even of those who are already Christian requires a missionary innovativeness, as it often does in times of change. Alas, the judgment of both higher church authorities and of the laity on pastors has too often been exclusively along the lines promoted by the Pastorals. The pastors who disturb because they see that new things have to be done, and those who are impatient over the inertia they encounter have frequently been rejected. So often churches work on what I call "the Caiaphas principle" when they encounter a brilliantly disturbing leader: It is better that one man be eliminated than that the whole institution perish (John 11:50). There may be a certain societal inevitability to that principle, but the source of it should at least make the designation "weakness" none too strong for a tendency (which is incipient in the Pastorals) to favor blandness.

Third, there are strengths and weaknesses in the church's having carefully selected presbyter-bishops who alone can hand on the doctrine safely, with the result that other teachers arouse suspicion. The plus and minus values are patent in II Tim 3:1–9, a passage that vituperates other teachers who oppose the authority of the presbyters and mislead people:

> [1]But understand this: in the last days there will come times of stress. [2]For people will be lovers of themselves, lovers of money, proud, arrogant, abusive, disobedient to their parents, ungrateful, unholy, [3]inhuman, unforgiving, slanderers, profligate, brutal, haters of good, [4]treacherous, rash, conceited, lovers of pleasure rather than lovers of God, [5]holding the form of religion but denying the power of it. Have nothing to do with such people. [6]For among them are those who make their way into households and gain control over weak women burdened with sins and swayed by various impulses, [7]who will listen to anybody and never arrive

at a knowledge of the truth. [8]As Jannes and Jambres opposed Moses, so also these oppose the truth—these people of depraved mind and counterfeit faith. [9]But they will not get very far, for their folly will be plain to all, as was that of those two men.

The vituperation is made up of customary, expected charges. The gnostic teachers under attack may well have deserved some of the descriptive adjectives; but not infrequently where only approved teachers flourish, those who ask probing questions about the standard doctrine will be presented as the opponents of God's truth. In other words, prompted by struggle, the Pastorals present a dualistic view of the true and the counterfeit, but ordinary church life is scarcely dualistic. Differing from standard teaching may indeed be a mark of false teachers who need to be opposed; it may also be a mark of constructive thinkers whose ideas, startling at first, may lead the appointed teachers to perceive more clearly what really has been entrusted to be guarded with the help of the Holy Spirit (II Tim 1:14). In the Roman Catholic Church the Galileo case is a notorious example of where the official teachers confused a new teaching with false teaching because involved was a different view, challenging what had always been taught from the Scriptures about the relation between the sun and the earth. One could find thousands of less famous examples, many of them in Protestantism; and they warn us that a condemnatory dualistic approach may be an example of weakness rather than of strength.

In regard to the II Tim 3 passage, however, I am more interested in the attitude of this passage towards those who are taught, for the author ungracefully refers to "weak women" as an example of the ignorant and impulsive who are easily misled. One may argue that he is not speaking about all women[61] and that in his time women were seldom given the opportunity of education. Meeks, *First Urban* 23–24, points out that conservative Greco-Roman historians and sat-

---

61. Elsewhere in the Pastorals "real widows" are honored (I Tim 5:3), and women deacons are envisioned (3:11). Elder women are to teach what is good (Titus 2:3) and to be treated with respect (I Tim 5:2—for the debatable suggestion that the latter are women presbyters, see the discussion in Brown, *Critical Meaning* 141). But the author permits no woman to teach or have authority over men (I Tim 2:12).

irists frequently blamed the lush growth of esoteric cults and super-
stitions on irresponsible women who felt emancipated by them.
Plutarch (*Moralia: Coniugalia praecepta* 145CE) observes that uneducated women tend to believe in superstitious stupidities, and unless
they receive the seeds of good doctrine, they conceive monstrosities.
Certainly some of the rules limiting women in the Pauline writings
are designed to show that Christians are not rebels against the social
expectations of the Hellenistic world, and are not a wild sect. Be that
as it may, II Tim 3:6–7 can easily contribute to a generalization
wherein women typify the taught section of the community who will
always get things wrong unless they are instructed by the official
teachers. Understandably, many modern readers or hearers will be
offended by what will appear to them as sexist; and preachers, instead of decrying such a reaction as simplistic or anchronistic, should
take the trouble to interpret the passage critically in both senses of
that adverb. Elsewhere[62] I have stated my firm opinion that little is
gained in public reading by omitting offensive Bible passages, for
bowdlerized versions permit people too easily to say they "accept"
the Bible. They never hear passages that should cause an intelligent
audience to demur and to ask themselves constructive questions that
will lead them to recognize the human conditioning in the biblical
account. Hearing the difficult passages of the Bible and wrestling with
them honestly (rather than explaining them away) will strengthen
the realization that every word spoken about God on this earth, including the biblical word, which is uniquely "of God," is a partial
and limited witness to the truth.[63] To accept the Bible in that sense
leads to a faith that is not credulous.

As part of the "wrestling" with this passage in II Timothy, I
would like to go beyond the unpleasant fact that women personify
the dangerously weak and naive in order to concentrate on the problem of *a class of those who are taught.* (I shall return to the Pastorals'
treatment of women in Chapter 7 below.) From the Pastorals one
gets the impression that officially appointed teachers and false teachers are battling for the minds of those who are to be taught. Some-

---

62. R. E. Brown, "The Passion According to John," *Worship* 49 (#3, March
1975) 131.
63. *Critical Meaning* (1–22) argues this point in detail.

times such a picture has been equated with the classical theological distinction between the *ecclesia docens* (teaching church) and the *ecclesia discens* (learning church). This is a valid distinction as long as one recognizes that membership in the two groups is mobile—at one time or other every Christian is or should be part of the teaching church and everyone should be part of the learning church.[64] However, from the Pastorals one might judge that, apart from the presbyters, everyone else is in a fixed class of the taught who, if not instructed by the official teachers, will be deceived by false teachers.[65]

Only the foolish would deny the danger that uneducated members of a Christian community will be deceived by false teachers. For instance, today there are many Roman Catholics (and increasingly many Protestants from the mainline churches) who have little acquaintance with the Bible from youth and whose first real familiarity with it comes through hearing fundamentalist media-preachers. How quickly they can be convinced by simplistic interpretations! But granted this, very often a greater peril faces the community where the dividing line between official teachers and the taught is very sharp, namely, the peril that little by way of creative ideas or intellectual contributions is expected from the taught who constitute the majority of the community. Certainly II Tim 3:6–7 shows no expectation that sometimes women might on their own detect a falsehood peddled to them or might even have something to teach the presbyters. The failure of the author to make allowance for ideas "from the bottom up," as if all perspicacity comes from the top down in the structure, does not prepare the ordinary readers of the Pastorals to play a contributive role in teaching. Such a one-sided situation will become ever more disastrous in any area of the world where the laity are highly educated and quite capable of making a significant contribution toward the overall religious growth of the community. Of course, even educated laity need to be taught the great Christian tradition, and that is a signal task of the official teachers of the church who have been (or should have been) trained in that tradition. But once having been instructed, some lay people are quite capable of be-

---

64. See *Critical Meaning* 47–48.
65. Footnote 61 above indicates that the author's thought was more subtle and made an allowance for familial teaching.

ing teachers themselves, not just transmitting what they received but making their own contribution. The Pastoral Epistles were written at a time when the author felt he had to tell Titus (3:1), "Remind the people to be submissive to rulers and authorities"; perhaps he expected the good sense that at another time it would be said, "Remind them to be constructive and contributive." But the fact is that such a follow-up directive never made it into the Scriptures that were to be so pastorally determinant. That is a weakness.

A need to insist that there are weaknesses in the Pastorals' proposal of firm administration by official teachers is a compliment to the enormous strength of that proposal, which has tended to dominate church history precisely because it worked so well. Communities that have reacted by ignoring it have often been short-lived. As we shall see in Chapter 7 below, the one NT community that specifically rejected the idea of official teachers lost many of its members, and the remnant ultimately had to accept a qualified form of pastoral authority.

CHAPTER 3

The Pauline Heritage in Colossians/Ephesians: The Church as Christ's Body to Be Loved

COLOSSIANS/EPHESIANS constitutes another strain of the sub-apostolic heritage, even more directly connected to Paul than were the Pastoral Epistles. Colossians may have been composed within a decade of Paul's lifetime, closer to him in time than any of the other Deutero-Pauline letters.[66] It has so many features of genuine Pauline thought (but not of Pauline style) that even some critical scholars think that Paul composed it, at least through a secretary. (By way of very broad approximation, about 90% of critical scholarship judges that Paul did not write the Pastorals, 80% that he did not write Ephesians, and 60% that he did not write Colossians.) It is not clear to what extent the author of Colossians knew the earlier Pauline

---

66. Ephesians is difficult to date but the period A.D. 90–100 is plausible. The tendency to place the Pastorals in the second century is debatable; and I would disagree with H.F. von Campenhausen and H. Koester who tend toward the mid-second century and would place the Pastorals at the same distance from Paul as Polycarp stands. See G. Lohfink in Kertelge, *Paulus* 119. Nevertheless, some decades separate the Paul of the 60s from the writing of the Pastorals (a possible implication of II Tim 1:5, if Paul is imagined as a contemporary of Timothy's grandmother). P. Trümmer, *Die Paulustradition der Pastoralbriefe* (Beiträge zur biblischen Exegese und Theologie 8; Frankfurt: Lang, 1978) speaks of writing in the third generation after Paul. Marcion's failure to acknowledge the Pastorals in his canon (if it represents ignorance of them rather than ignoring) and their absence from P[46] may indicate that they were preserved differently from the rest of the Pauline collection.

writings (beyond Philemon), but the author of Ephesians knew most of them.[67] However, beyond stressing that both Colossians and Ephesians belong to the Pauline heritage, let me leave such details to NT Introductions (ftnote 19 above) and concentrate on the basic question I am posing to all the sub-apostolic works: Granted that the apostolic figure has passed (or is passing) from the scene, how do these writings enable the communities addressed to survive?[68]

As in the Pastorals, so also in Colossians/Ephesians, Paul gives authoritative apostolic guidance.[69] As in I Tim 3:15, so also in Eph 2:19 we hear of the church as the "household of God"; and the institutional aspect of this image is strengthened in the next verse which speaks of being "built upon the foundation of the apostles and prophets, with Christ Jesus himself as the cornerstone." In both Colossians and Ephesians instructions for the ethical behavior of members of the Christian household (Haustafeln) are supplied in a manner not far removed from similar instructions in the Pastorals. An awareness of a charismatic church structure is exhibited by Eph 4:11 which lists apostles, prophets, evangelists, pastors, and teachers. Yet, unlike the author of the Pastorals, the authors of Colossians and Ephesians put no stress on apostolic succession or on the institutional aspects of the church. We hear nothing significant about the functioning of the "pastors and teachers." The silence cannot be explained on the grounds of a trouble-free situation. Colossians 2:8–23 describes vividly the onslaught of false teaching which consists of a "human tradition . . . not according to Christ." In it Jewish elements are mixed with aspects of a visionary mystery religion, and one gets the impression of error no less serious than what is condemned in the Pastorals.

---

67. The extent to which the author of the Pastorals knew the other Pauline Epistles has been debated but the relationship between the two sets of writings is not purely literary.

68. As noted in ftnote 21 above, for the purposes of this question it is possible to treat the two epistles together. Yet to be precise, the ecclesiology of Ephesians goes beyond that of Colossians. Good on this point is H. Merklein, "Paulinische Theologie in der Rezeption des Kolosser- und Epheserbriefes," in Kertelge, Paulus 25-69, esp. 58–62 where he points out that even the cross has become ecclesiological in Ephesians. He challenges Käsemann's thesis that in Ephesians christology has ceded to ecclesiology; rather Ephesians presents "an ecclesiological christology."

69. Eph 2:20; 3:5; and 4:11 speak of "apostles" in the plural; but in Eph 3:1–13, which contains references to Paul's career, clearly Paul as the apostolic "I" dominates the picture.

False teaching problems are mentioned in more general language in Ephesians,[70] e.g. in 4:14 which warns against being children "blown about by every wind of doctrine and by human cunning and craftiness in deceitful scheming."

Rather than responding to such doctrinal dangers by emphasis on appointed teachers and transmitted doctrine, Colossians offers a positive, idealistic view of the church, which is expanded in Ephesians. In the undisputed letters of Paul we find him using "church" frequently but most often in reference to local communities,[71] e.g., "the church of God which is in Corinth," "the churches of Galatia," "in every church." But in Colossians/Ephesians the absolute, comprehensive term "*the* church" has come to the fore. Then as now, "the church" used absolutely is hard to define, for it is more than the aggregate of individual churches or Christian communities. Indeed, as will become clear, in Colossians/Ephesians "the church" seems to be more than an earthly reality, for it affects the heavenly powers—a foreshadowing of the expansion in later theology to a church triumphant (in heaven) alongside a church militant (on earth), and, in Roman Catholicism, alongside a church suffering (in purgatory).

Paul had resorted to an imaginative use of Christ's "body" in his undisputed correspondence, especially in overcoming the jealousy about charisms at Corinth. He spoke of the risen body of Christ (and thus of a real body that had lived and died) of which each Christian is a member,[72] a human body that had feet, hands, eyes, etc. Paul used this diversity of bodily parts to justify the difference in charisms enjoyed by the Corinthian Christians: some prophets, some healers, some speakers in tongues (I Cor 12:21–31). The author of Colossians, followed by the author of Ephesians, adopts Paul's image of the body and develops it in a new way to fit a massive emphasis on

---

70. The sections in Colossians that attack a specific error are not repeated in Ephesians, a work that is only marginally a letter and may not have been addressed to a specific church. Ephesians has the air of being a universal instruction consisting of a generalized Pauline message interpreted through the ecclesiology of Colossians.

71. There are a few instances indicating that a more comprehensive use of the term was not foreign to Paul: I Cor 12:28: "God has appointed in the church first apostles, second prophets . . ."; I Cor 15:9; Gal 1:13: "I persecuted the church."

72. See also Rom 12:4–5. The chain of ideas is that through baptism each Christian becomes identified with him who died and rose. "You have died to the Law through the body of Christ" (Rom 7:4).

the church.[73] In his body of the flesh by his death Christ reconciled those who were estranged (Col 1:21), and they have been called into one body (3:15). That body is now identified as the church, and Christ is its head (Col 1:18,24; Eph 1:22–23; 5:23). From Paul's reference to the Christians as members of a real body that suffered, died, and rose, the thrust of the body imagery has moved to a corporate understanding with Christ as Lord over that body (Eph 4:4–5).

Despite the corporate understanding, the church as the body of Christ does not become a corporation. Here is a major difference from the Pastorals[74] where the care in setting up authoritative administration inevitably has underscored the institutional. For Colossians/Ephesians the church is a growing entity, living with the life of Christ himself. The basic error is to lose "connection to the head from whom the whole body, nourished and knit together through its joints and ligaments, grows with a growth that is from God" (Col 2:19). If there are different ministries, they are "for building up the body of Christ, until we all reach ... to the measure of the stature of the fullness of Christ" (Eph 4:12–13). "We are to grow in every way into him who is the head, that is, into Christ from whom the whole body, joined and knit together by every joint, ... grows bodily and builds itself up in love" (Eph 4:15–16).

In this approach to the church, the theme of love is very strong. In the undisputed correspondence of Paul, he wished to present the Corinthians to Christ as a pure virgin to a husband. This imagery has

---

73. Even so did the author of the Pastorals develop strains of thought about pastoral authority encountered in the undisputed letters of Paul, e.g., I Thess 5:12; Philip 1:1. In each case the development is innovative, but the line that is developed comes authentically from Paul. We are seeing different "trajectories" in the Pauline heritage. Meeks, *First Urban* 8, would challenge this for the Pastorals, for he doubts that they are products of a Pauline school. Paul is simply adopted as a convenient patron, and the Pastorals "cannot be used with any confidence, either as evidence of any sort of social continuity or as independent testimony to any traditions of the Pauline groups."

74. Note: I do not speak of a contradiction. Formally, there is no way of knowing whether the authors of Colossians/Ephesians were aware of the Pastorals, or vice versa. Conzelmann, "Die Schule" 88, points out that if one speaks of a post-Pauline school, there are no cross-references from one writer to the other (except, of course, for the author of Ephesians using Colossians). Internally, the emphasis in Colossians/Ephesians on the Body of Christ is not incompatible with the existence of church administration.

been expanded in Ephesians to a relationship between Christ and "the church." Indeed, Eph 5:21–33 does not hesitate to pattern the love between husband and wife on the intense love of Christ for the church. (If church order in the Pastorals is patterned on the administration of a household, in Ephesians the ideals of the household are patterned on the church.) Christ nourishes and cherishes the church (5:29). "Christ loved the church and gave himself up for her" (5:25). The latter statement may be contrasted to statements in II Cor 5:14 and in Rom 5 that Christ died for all, indeed for the unrighteous and sinners. The goal of Christ's life and death has become the church. Even more, the church may be said to be the ultimate goal of God's master plan, since all things in heaven and on earth have been put under Christ's feet and he has been made "head over all things *for the church* which is his body" (Eph 1:22–23). The mystery or hidden plan of God involves Christ's love for the church (Eph 5:32 and what precedes).

Holiness is a very important characteristic of the church as the body of Christ. He died to sanctify the church and to cleanse her that she might be presented as a "radiant bride without spot or wrinkle or any such thing, that she might be holy and without blemish" (Eph 5:27). The two become one (5:31–32) so that the holiness of Christ may be seen in the church, his body that is being built up in love (4:16). Indeed, the church can be identified with the kingdom of God's Son. There is much insistence in introductory NT courses that *hē basileia tou theou* (the kingdom of God) is an active, not a static or localized concept, and would be translated better as "rule, reign," not "kingdom." A corollary often drawn is that the initiation of the rule of God by Jesus cannot simply be equated with the founding of the church. In such observations, true as they may be, one must not overlook the fact that in some of the later sections of the NT *basileia* has been reified and localized, so that "kingdom" is the only appropriate translation. One enters it, and there are keys to it. Also the kingdom and the church have begun to be partially identified.

Important in this regard is Matthew's explanation of the parable about the weeds planted and allowed to grow among the wheat (13:36–43). The good seed are the sons of the kingdom; the weeds are the sons of the evil one; when the harvest comes, "the Son of

Man will send his angels, and they will gather *out of his kingdom* all
the causes of sin and all evildoers. . . . Then the righteous will shine
like the sun in the kingdom of their Father." Thus there is a kingdom of the Son of Man on earth with good and bad—seemingly the
church—but only after the judgment will the just enter the kingdom
of their Father. Colossians may be even more radical in equating the
church with a form of the kingdom: the Father "has rescued us from
the dominion of darkness and transferred us into the kingdom of His
beloved Son in whom we have redemption and the forgiveness of
sins" (1:13–14).[75] Thus the darkness-free church of which Christians
are members is the kingdom of God's Son in which "they share the
inheritance of the holy ones in the light" (1:12). This is possible because, as part of the realized eschatology of Colossians/Ephesians,
Christians are told, "You were raised in Christ through faith" (Col
2:12). Another passage (Col 3:1–3) indicates that heavenly glory is
still future; but Eph 2:6 sees even this aspect too as partially realized:
God "raised us up with him and seated us with him in the heavenly
places in Christ Jesus."[76]

When, as cited above, Colossians speaks of Christians' sharing
"the inheritance of the holy ones in the light," it is likely that these
holy ones are not just saintly human beings of the past but the angels; for Christ has reconciled all things on earth and in heaven (Col
1:20; Eph 1:10), and the powers and principalities are subject to him
who is the head of the church. Thus, in a sense the angelic, superhu-

---

75. Colossians 4:11 mentions "fellow-workers for the kingdom of God," and
Eph 5:5 refers to "the kingdom of Christ and of God"; but it is not clear whether two
kingdoms or stages of the kingdom are envisioned (as in Matthew), nor whether the
church can be identified with the kingdom of God. Even in Eph (1:14) there is an inheritance which we have not yet acquired.

76. Paul in I Thess 4:14; Rom 6:5; and Philip 3:10–12 regards the resurrection
of the Christian from the dead as something future. The tendency to regard resurrection and even ascension into heaven as having taken place for the Christian is a step
leading to gnosticism. The Valentinian, Nag Hammadi gnostic author of the *Treatise
on the Resurrection to Rheginos* (I 45:24–28) writes: "As the apostle said, 'We suffered
with him; we ascended to heaven with him.' " (Notice how the "Pauline" position has
been extended and hardened even beyond Ephesians.) That is why II Tim 2:18 con-
demns those "who have wandered from the truth by claiming that the resurrection is
already past." Nevertheless, there are passages even in the undisputed letters of Paul
that may have sparked such a movement toward realized eschatology, e.g., Rom 5:18
where Christ's act of righteousness is said to lead to *life* for all, and Rom 8:24, "For in
this hope we were saved."

man powers who acknowledge Christ may be considered part of the church as the body of Christ. Like a Byzantine mosaic picturing the Pantocrator, the body and the head reach from earth to heaven. If Col 2:9 can state that the fullness of divinity dwells in Christ bodily, Eph 1:23 can simplify this by describing the church as "his body, the fullness of Him who fills all in all"; and this fullness may well include the angels. If Paul described himself as a servant/minister *(diakonos)* of God (II Cor 6:4), and of a new covenant (II Cor 3:6), it is not surprising that the "Paul" of Col 1:24–25 can describe himself as a servant/minister *of the church.* The doxology of Eph 3:21 indicates the extent to which these letters have given an almost divine character to the church: "To Him be glory in the church and in Christ Jesus to all generations for ever and ever."[77]

STRENGTHS AND WEAKNESSES

Having described the exalted ecclesiology of Colossians/Ephesians, I now turn to the way in which it relates to the survival of the churches the apostle Paul left behind. **First,** we have seen that the body of Christ imagery personalizes the church and encourages our love for it in imitation of the love that Christ has for his bride. The advice given by the Pastorals should produce an efficient, caring administration; but ultimately people do not love a structure or an institution in itself. Let me illustrate a personal and an institutional image from current experience. In my own church, before the Second Vatican Council one heard frequently the language of "mother church." Admittedly that imagery smacked of over-supervision and of a maternalism that reduced everyone to a child status, or at times to a childish status. In part, such weakness explains why the imagery is no longer very popular; yet no real replacement has been found. Post-Vatican II references to "the institutional church" often em-

---

77. A further, gnostic development of this is seen in Valentinus who makes *ekklēsia,* "church," an eon in the schema of divine emanations. On the cosmic character of restoration in this branch of the Pauline heritage and its implications, see W. A. Meeks, "In One Body: The Unity of Humankind in Colossians and Ephesians," in *God's Christ and His People,* ed. J. Jervell and W. A. Meeks (Nils A. Dahl Festschrift; Oslo: Universitetsforlaget, 1977) 209–21.

body the misunderstanding that there are two churches of which one is non-institutional. (The church is by nature social and implicitly institutional. Those who "opt out of the institutional church" may continue with private religion, but they are no longer in union with the church as it exists on this earth. If they join a small group or sect that presents itself as non-institutional, it will soon become institutional provided it lasts long enough and gains a sizable membership.) But even when references to "the institutional church" do not involve such a misunderstanding, they scarcely reflect warmth or passionate admiration. Institution or structure is inevitably influenced by secular models and constitutes that aspect of the church which is not easily seen as having anything to do with Christ or God. For all its defects, "mother church" was both personal and familial; and even when a mother overdoes her role, she can be loved by her children.

One implication of a personal church conceived as the body loved by Christ is seen in a statement attributed to Paul: "What is lacking in Christ's afflictions I complete in my flesh for the sake of his body which is the church" (Col 1:24). This is an attitude derivative from the principle that Christ "gave himself up for her" (Eph 5:25). If Christ was willing to give himself for the church, so should his apostle be willing to give himself for the church. And once the apostle has passed from the scene, if there are still others who are willing to give themselves for the church, the church will survive. People, since they do not love institutions as such, rarely give themselves for institutions; rather institutions exist for people. But if the church is loved in a personalized relationship, it becomes a cause that attracts generosity from generation to generation.

A moment's reflection easily supplies examples of this through the centuries. The cathedrals, which were the dominant edifices of medieval cities, were built with great sacrifices by people who expressed their love for God and Christ by what they did for such a church. Immigrants to the U.S.A. often built great churches and cathedrals while they themselves were housed in poor circumstances. The church building was to them a sign of continuity with the tradition and faith they had known as children in their native countries. How often men and women have left a good part of their life savings simply "to the church"! In Roman Catholicism those who became priests, or brothers, or sisters were commonly said to have given their lives "to the church." I suspect that this last mentioned instance of "to the church" language may be foreign to many Protestants, but it is a logical derivative from the ecclesiology of Colossians/Ephesians which tends to make the church and Christ one.

Second, the holiness of the church that is part of the Colossians/Ephesians picture is also an element that enables the church to survive. Inevitably church members sin; already in Paul's lifetime marriage disputes, incest, and profanation of the eucharist marred the church at Corinth. In the communities addressed by the Pastorals, the carefully chosen presbyter-bishops might correct and even prevent some of those stains on the sanctity of the local church; but they themselves were open to sin. (Money and power are two principal values in this world; and it would be a sociological miracle if church institutions, inescapably patterned on surrounding institutions, would not be tempted to take over such values.) It is no accident that NT directives to presbyters warn explicitly or implicitly against greed and arrogant domination (I Peter 5:2–3; Acts 20:32–35). Sinful scandals imperil the survival of the church unless people have an appreciation of its holiness that is not destroyed by individual sins. The author of Ephesians knew many of the undisputed Pauline Epistles and consequently knew that scandals existed in churches founded and supervised by the great apostle. Yet he could write of *the church* as a spotless bride, holy and without blemish. His appreciation of the church was not naive romanticism but mystical vision. Those who follow his example will be able to acknowledge sins and still put them into perspective through love for the church. Institutional scandals and stupidities, even at the highest administrative levels, will not prevent people with this vision from completing "what is lacking in Christ's afflictions for the sake of his body, that is, the church" (Col 1:24). In the Apostles' Creed there is a clause "I believe in the holy catholic church." As long as people have that faith, the church will last, no matter how inefficient its administration.

Thus far I have been underlining the strong points of the ecclesiastical imagery of Colossians/Ephesians. Now let us look at the weak points. **First** and paradoxically, an emphasis on the holiness of the church can be a weakness if it begins to mask faults that exist.

Sometimes an ecclesiology of holiness has led Christians to hide sins
or stupidities, especially those of public church figures, on the
grounds that scandal would be caused if they were known. I am not
speaking of hypocritical suppression by those who are guilty but suppression by the innocent out of love. Just as a husband or wife will
not proclaim the spouse's faults to all the world because of loyalty
and love for the family, so the thought that the church is Christ's
body or spouse whom Christ loves has led to silence about what
could mar the image of that church. Yet oppression, venality, and
dishonesty harm the inner vitality of the church; and they may need
to be exposed and spoken against. Silence may prolong the harm
done to Christians who suffer under such sins. Moreover, where suppression has occurred for a long period, Christians are not being
taught to deal maturely with the tension that surrounds a spotless
church filled with sinners. Consequently, when the dam of silence ultimately breaks (and break it will), the disillusionment can be cata-
strophic.

If I may take the Roman Catholic Church as an example, the
period before Vatican II was characterized by a public silence about
faults, especially about those of the clergy and religious. I trust that
no one will accuse us of that fault recently. Now it seems as if the
front page of a newspaper is the only forum for dealing with inner-
Catholic difficulties! The dubious service that the *National Enquirer*
renders to the nation, the *National Catholic Reporter* renders to the
church. The very sharpness of this change demonstrates vividly the
pent-up feelings flowing from such artificial silence—it may even
cause people to forget the gospel maxim that first one should remon-
strate in private and only reluctantly go public (Matt 18:15–17).
Even worse, now that a flood of scandalous secrets has been made
known (and, to be honest, exaggerated), many Catholic people are
not able to cope with the discovery that greed, pride, and even sex
were at work in a church which previously they had not seen criti-
cized in "black and white" from within. (Yes, there had been printed
criticism from outsiders, but they could be dismissed as enemies.) So
often the reaction to the unpleasant revelations is that, if this is the
way the church really is, I want no part of it. If money has been mis-
used or badly invested, why should I give to the church? If church
positions on complicated issues, including papal encyclicals, repre-

sent compromises between feuding factions rather than universal consent among top church advisors, why am I to give adherence? If priests and sisters are leaving their ministry and revealing the frustrations present in the public service of the church, why should anyone undertake such service by way of vocation?

Such objections, heard so frequently today (and not only among Roman Catholics), are a contemporary expression of a problem encountered in another form in the early church. Paul is eloquent in I Cor 1:23: "We preach Christ crucified, a scandal to the Jews and folly to the Gentiles." The Christ of Paul would not have been a scandal if he were shown as representing God without any human admixture. The Christ of Paul would not have been a folly if he were shown as a purely human embodiment of God-like virtues. But the mixture of the divine and the human in christology constituted the scandal and the folly. Who could believe that the power of God was embodied in one who was hanged as a criminal? Who could believe in a salvific figure dying on a cross, an image as palatable as a hunk of meat hanging in a butcher shop, covered with blood, dirt, and flies? When one describes the crucifixion in such graphic terms, even contemporary Christians feel for a moment the offense of Paul's preaching; but the cross or crucifix has been too long a reverential symbol for it to constitute a scandal. So where is the scandal in the Christian gospel today? Not in Christ crucified but in the church. (The parallel is not perfect: there was no sin in Christ himself; there is sin in those who constitute the church.) When faults are concealed, the church may not be a scandal; but let the narrowness, the abuse of power, the stupidities, venalities, and sins be known, and the cry of scandal and folly that greeted Paul's gospel will greet the creedal proclamation, "I believe in the holy, catholic church." A generation that on the political level demands the simon-pure and that expects leaders on white chargers will be "turned off" by the claim that the vehicle for Christ's salvific message is a church with such human tarnish. They will dismiss the church as just another political organization, and run off after a "pure cause." Nevertheless, a church where the holiness has to be perceived in faith but where the faults are physically visible embodies the mystery of the divine in the human— the very mystery that constituted the offensive Pauline gospel. An exclusive concentration on holiness (which may result from reading

Ephesians without the author's presuppositions based on his knowledge of the Pauline corpus) can become a vehicle of gnosticism rather than of the gospel.

A **second** weakness in this ecclesiology concerns the possibility
of reform. It is difficult to think of reforming a spotless bride. If the
members of a body are being knit together in growth that comes
from God and are being upbuilt in love, is there place for defective
and cancerous growths, for sickness, and for corrective operations?
Does the inherent triumphalism of Colossians/Ephesians allow for
failure? To express the difficulty more concretely, is not this view of
the church, especially in Ephesians, logically more consistent with a
"high catholicism" such as found in the Eastern Churches, Roman
Catholicism, and Anglicanism than with the ecclesiology of the Protestant Reformation? K. Lake, *Landmarks* 93, remarks bluntly,
"Protestant scholarship is more sensitive to the un-Pauline ecclesiology of Ephesians, which it repudiates, than to the un-Pauline Christology of Colossians, to which it adheres." If the Reformers were
correct in their thesis that the Roman Church had become hopeless-
ly corrupt and if the style of that Church to which they objected had
existed for many centuries, how is that reconcilable with the thesis in
Eph 5 that Christ had sanctified and cleansed the church and that
the two had become one? If Ephesians and Colossians are correct,
can there be an essentially corrupt visible church? A frequent Protestant answer to such an objection is that, after a gap, the Reformed
Churches were the true successors of an earlier, incorrupt church.[78]
This answer, which may seem incredible to Roman Catholics, really
proves the power of the ecclesiology of Colossians/Ephesians. Every
group, even if it posits massive corruption, will suppose that in some
period the church was substantially pure. Perhaps the Church of the
Latter Day Saints (Mormons) is the most extreme example of this,
for it posits that the "great apostasy" took place in the first century
and that divine revelation to Joseph Smith recovered the uncorrupt
church.

This basic difficulty about the thrust of Colossians/Ephesians
may be brought home to Roman Catholics by reflections on Vatican

---

78. Obviously there are other and more sophisticated Protestant answers to this
"high catholic" objection.

II, a self-reform council where the Roman Church accomplished from within, by its own decision, some of what the Reformers had attempted from without, by protest. In the years before the council the dominant biblical image of the church for Catholics had become the body of Christ. The encyclical on the Mystical Body by Pope Pius XII (1943) had the effect of challenging a purely canonical understanding of the church in terms of jurisdiction. The Pope's presentation was largely informed by the basic imagery of Colossians/Ephesians, even if the encyclical already, by its title with the word "mystical," went beyond the Bible. If a poll on biblical church imagery had been taken among bishops entering the council, the "body of Christ" would surely have won first place in familiarity. But that is not the biblical imagery that emerged from the council.[79] Dominating post-conciliar Roman Catholic ecclesiology is a biblical image that would rarely have been mentioned in preconciliar sermons, namely, the people of God. Why? An important but partial answer is found in the different thrusts of the body of Christ and the people of God. The awesome holiness of the body of Christ which is the spotless bride did not lend itself to self-reform. Indeed, Catholic resistance to the reforms of Vatican II was often based on the thesis that such changes implied previous church error or fault. And so, perhaps without adverting to the dynamism of the shift, the council facilitated reform by turning to the image of the people of God—a people that is unique because it is of God and yet may still consist of sinners; a pilgrim people on its way to the promised land, wandering at times and needing to be brought back from detours. This image was needed alongside the body of Christ in order to give expression to the tension in ecclesiology between holiness and the constant need for reform.

As for the last two possible weaknesses in the ecclesiology of Colossians/Ephesians, let me be brief because they really are not pertinent to the survival of the church after the death of the apostles. A **third** weakness is that the emphasis on *the* church in these epistles weakens the role of local churches in ecclesiology. In Roman Catholicism this trend was so dominant over the centuries that the theology

---

79. I do not mean that the image of the body of Christ was either rejected or disappeared, but it did lose its dominance.

of the local church is almost a new area.[80] Rather than speaking of a local church, we tend to speak of a parish or diocese, and to apply the term "church" without a qualifier to the universal entity. Ask the ordinary Catholic believers where is the center of their church, and most often the answer given will be "Rome." Yet in a very real way the church finds its center when the believing community celebrates a liturgy in which the word of God is being preached and the eucharist is being received. Without losing the concept of *the* church, those shaped by Colossians/Ephesians need to work with the holiness of the local community. On the local level the knitting together of the members is badly needed.

Fourth, an exclusive concentration on the church as the ultimate goal of God's plan of salvation in Christ omits from explicit consideration a large part of the world that is not yet renewed in Christ. In this outlook, only as part of the body of Christ is there cosmic unity. The hostile role of the principalities, powers, and rulers of this world is acknowledged warningly (Eph 6:12); but there is no real consideration given to the many in this world who are neither believing nor hostile. True, a failure to deal with a "third world" that is neither light nor darkness is common in the NT; it is simply more apparent in the ecclesiology of Colossians/Ephesians.

Lest I end this section on a negative note, I wish to reaffirm the tremendous power of the Colossians/Ephesians ecclesiology with its elements of holiness and love. No church can survive without giving it due emphasis. Inevitably, after their strong condemnation of the Roman Church, the Reformers applied the body of Christ imagery to the reformed churches that emerged from their protest. The sixteenth century churches were seen by their adherents as the true heirs to the title of the spotless bride that Christ had cleansed and sanctified. Within Roman Catholicism, if we have another decade of the dominance of the people of God imagery, the body of Christ motif will need to re-emerge. After all, Israel was (and, for many, still is) the people of God. What is distinctive about the Christian church is the relationship to Christ and the special holiness that has flowed from that relationship.

---

80. See my article cited in ftnote 24 above.

CHAPTER 4

The Pauline Heritage in Luke/Acts: The Church and the Spirit

As indicated above (p. 20), Luke/Acts constitutes another form of the Pauline heritage, even though the author shows no knowledge of the Epistles.[81] The Lucan Paul is a more moderate figure than the Paul who wrote Galatians and the Corinthian correspondence. For some scholars this is a falsification of Paul; yet Paul was not a monolothic character, and there would have been a tendency to recall selectively the more benevolent and pacific aspects of his career, especially after the martyred apostle had become a pillar of the church (*I Clement* 5:2–5).[82]

A work like Acts is not an apt parallel in form or in content to the Pastorals or to Colossians/Ephesians, and so we must move cautiously in evaluating its contribution to post-Pauline ecclesiolgy. Unlike the authors of those other works, the author of Acts has not written a work of Pauline theology; he has written a story in which Paul plays a decisive role as a missionary witness, not as a doctrinal authority. Scholars are far from agreement on the audience addressed in Acts,[83] an audience that may have been less specified than

---

81. On this point, consult the balanced judgment of Barrett, "Acts."

82. See Donfried, *Word* 71–75.

83. P.-G. Müller, in Kertelge, *Paulus* 156–201, argues that the circumstances of the milieu in which Luke received the Pauline tradition may be more important than the audience addressed.

the addressees of the Epistles. Nevertheless, we can work with the likelihood that Luke was working with largely Gentile churches[84] affected at least indirectly by the Pauline mission.

Even though we use the name "Luke," there are many reasons for thinking that the author was not a companion of Paul and had not known him personally.[85] Perhaps not even the audience had been in direct contact with the historical Paul. But for the author and presumably for the audience, Paul was an extremely important figure in God's plan to bring Christ to the Gentiles and to the ends of the earth. Paul had become the guarantor of the legitimacy of these Gentile churches. While the purpose of Luke/Acts may be complex, it certainly involves the basic geographic line traced in Acts 1:8, which constitutes the table of contents of the book: "You shall receive power when the Holy Spirit has come upon you, and you shall be my witnesses in Jerusalem, and all Judea and Samaria, and to the ends of the earth." Acts begins in Jerusalem, moves through Judea and Samaria, and ends in Rome. Personified in Peter and Paul at almost equal length, witness to Jesus is borne before Jews and Gentiles alike during the first three decades of Christian life (early 30s to the early 60s). The account was written decades later;[86] and one may debate the accuracy of the report and to what extent sources were available to the writer. But those questions need not concern us as we ask how Luke/Acts would help a Christian audience to survive the death of the apostles.

---

84. Impressed by Luke's emphasis that many Jews found Jesus credible and by his generally non-hostile description even of Jews who were not believers (e.g., Gamaliel), some scholars have argued that Luke must have been writing for Jewish Christians in whole or in part. They do not recognize that Luke describes a progressive Christian history in which dealings with the Jews are past. While there was no contradiction between Jesus and Judaism, as some Jews recognized, the contemporary situation for Luke is expressed in the closing lines of Acts (28:25–28): The Jews will never understand; their eyes are closed; the salvation of God has been sent to the Gentiles. See my *Birth of the Messiah* (Garden City, NY: Doubleday, 1977) 236–37.

85. I remind the reader that nothing in Luke/Acts identifies the author. The thesis that he was Luke, the companion of Paul mentioned in Philem 24; Col 4:14; and II Tim 4:11, is the product of late second-century scholarship. When that thesis is challenged by twentieth-century scholarship, it is an academic not a religious question.

86. A date in the 80s is very commonly proposed, although some distinguished critics (Haenchen, Conzelmann) opt for the turn of the first century.

Acts uses the term "church" for local churches, and certainly one finds in this book none of the church mysticism that pervades Colossians/Ephesians. Nevertheless, the author has been acclaimed the theologian par excellence of the one, holy, catholic, and apostolic church, since every one of those features marks the Christian life he describes. The author made a bold ecclesial step when he enlarged the story of Jesus' ministry and death that Mark 1:1 called "the Gospel of Jesus Christ," not only by rewriting and developing the Jesus story, but also by adding a second book concerning early Christianity. He was putting together on the same level the story of the proclamation of the kingdom by Jesus and the story of the proclamation of Jesus by Peter and Paul.[87] This means that the good news or gospel[88] concerns not only what God has done in Jesus but also what He has done in the Spirit.

This step resulted in a major characteristic of Lucan ecclesiology, *a sense of continuity* wherein the church is closely related to what went before. First, it is clear that church beginnings are related to Jesus himself. The Jesus who on Easter night ascended into heaven, bringing the Third Gospel to an end (Luke 24:51), is restored to the earthly scene at the beginning of Acts, so that clearly he introduces all that follows. This risen Jesus offers a partial answer to the relationship between the kingdom and the church which we saw discussed both in Matthew and in Colossians (p. 51 above). When asked whether at this time he would restore the kingdom, the risen Jesus replies that it is not given to the apostles to know the time, but that they should bear witness over the whole earth. An essential question that tortured early Christians has thus been answered in a way that ever afterwards the larger churches will make their own against sectarians, namely, in the Christian balance more attention is due to bearing witness to what Jesus has done than to expecting his coming. This answer by Jesus makes church existence

---

87. In a sense the subsequent church has undone what Luke intended by its canonical arrangement whereby Luke becomes a gospel alongside Mark, while Acts stands off by itself, unrelated to the gospel.

88. Luke prefers the verb *euangelizesthai* to the noun *euangelion* to describe the proclamation of the good news.

both explicable and essential until the coming of the kingdom.[89] It also makes intelligible why Luke is writing a book describing that existence.

But the continuity does not depend only on Jesus. Although Luke's book gained the title of "Acts of the Apostles," the title is not really accurate, for Luke never stresses that Paul is an apostle. Yet the title does underline the role played by identified leaders in the story. People who were with Jesus during the public ministry (the Twelve, the women, his mother and brothers) come over into early Christian life to insure the continuity Jesus wanted. Paul was not one of those, but he was commissioned by the risen Jesus; and later Peter and James certified the correctness of Paul's radical missionary decision to convert communities of Gentiles without demanding circumcision. Thus, not only are the early stages of church life continuous with Jesus, but also the later stages represented by Paul are continuous with the early stages represented by Peter.[90] If Peter does the same kind of miracles that Jesus did, Paul then does the same kind of miracles that Peter did. The sermons that Peter and Paul preach are remarkably similar, as a sign of a continous message as well as a continuous power. As for the later period after Paul will be gone, Paul has appointed presbyters in each church (Acts 14:23). When he parts from the Eastern mission-field for the last time, he urges the presbyters of Ephesus: "Keep watch over all the flock in which the Holy Spirit has made you overseers [bishops] to care for the church of God which he obtained with the blood of His own Son" (20:28). Thus a continuity beyond Paul is envisioned.[91]

Moreover, the continuity covers an ever greater span than from the sub-apostolic presbyters back to Jesus (through Paul and Peter). Jesus and the church stand in continuity with the whole tradition of

---

89. La Verdiere, "Communities" 589: "The Church's mission does not represent an absolute reality completely understandable in itself, but one which is relative to the prior historical life of Jesus, as well as to his future coming."

90. K. Löning, in Kertelge, *Paulus* 202–34, points out that Luke has made all the early church authorities spokesmen for justification by faith and thus "Paulinized" them.

91. Here Acts comes close to the Pastoral Epistles, but one does not find the deposit-of-faith motif clearly expounded in Acts. Moreover, for Acts "continuity" is a more exact term than "apostolic succession," which fits the Pastorals.

Israel.[92] In commenting on the Lucan infancy narratives (*Birth of the Messiah* 242–43), I have contended that Zechariah, Elizabeth, Simeon, and Anna are figures patterned on OT models who are brought forward from the story of Israel to meet Jesus. The characters in Luke 1–2 who accept Jesus are pious Jews, and everything is done according to the Law (1:6; 2:22–27,37,39), even as the earliest Christians in Acts are faithful to the piety of Israel (2:46; 3:1; 5:42). The Spirit of God that moved the prophets of Israel is conspicuously active in a prophetic way at the beginning of the story of Jesus (Luke 1:15,35,41,67,80; 2:25–27) and at the beginning of the church (Acts 1:8,16; 2:4,17). The line of continuity running smoothly through Israel, Jesus, Peter, and Paul is admirably summed up by Paul[93] in Acts 24:14: "I admit to you that according to the Way [i.e., the way taught by Jesus which may have served as a name for the Christian movement] . . . , I worship the God of our fathers. I believe everything that is laid down by the Law or is written in the prophets."

I have mentioned that for Luke the Spirit plays a connective role between the prophecy of Israel and the prophetic activity surrounding the birth of Jesus and the birth of the church. Indeed, the distinguishing feature of Lucan ecclesiology is the overshadowing presence of *the Spirit.* The 70 times that *pneuma,* "spirit," occurs in Acts constitute almost one-fifth of the total NT usages of that word.[94] Some have suggested that the second Lucan book could have been named more appropriately the Acts of the Spirit rather than the Acts of the Apostles. The fact that Luke omits all further reference to Peter, the great apostle, after the meeting at Jerusalem in Acts 15

---

92. J. A. Fitzmyer, *The Gospel According to Luke (I–IX)* (Garden City, NY: Doubleday, 1981) 9, argues that Luke's purpose was to write a continuation of biblical history, with Christianity as the logical and legitimate continuation of Judaism.

93. Obviously here Luke's own way of thinking has colored the image of Paul. The Paul of Galatians makes an apocalyptic contrast between curse/sin before Christ and grace/adoption after Christ. The Paul of Rom 9 – 11 speaks a language closer to that of continuity. Such differences within Paul are why I favor the view that Luke has simplified selectively genuine aspects of the historical Paul. I would not agree entirely with the harmonious outlook of F. F. Bruce, "Is the Paul of Acts the Real Paul?" *Bulletin John Rylands Library* 58 (1976) 283–305; but his valid points warn against creating too deep a chasm between the two views of Paul.

94. See my article "Diverse Views of the Spirit in the New Testament," *Worship* 57 (#3, May 1983) 225–36.

and never tells about Peter's subsequent career or death has puzzled many. Even more disconcerting is that Acts closes when Paul gets to Rome and there is no reference to his subsequent career and death. (The inaccurate deduction that the book must have been written while Paul was alive stems from a failure to notice the parallelism with Peter.) Luke is not interested in these men as such, but in them as vehicles of the Spirit, bearing witness to Christ in Jerusalem, Judea, Samaria, and to the ends of the earth. The Spirit is the main actor.

In the two sets of post-Pauline works considered thus far, the Holy Spirit is assigned relatively little ecclesiological role. As part of a total 7 instances of *pneuma* in the Pastorals,[95] mention is made of regeneration by the Spirit in baptism (Titus 3:5) and of the entrusting of the truth to be guarded with the help of the indwelling Spirit (II Tim 1:14)—both common, traditional Christian ideas. The reference to the Spirit that really matters for the ecclesiology of the Pastorals is found in II Tim 1:6–7 where "Paul" reminds Timothy "to rekindle the gift of God that is in you through the laying on of my hands, for God did not give us a spirit of timidity, but a Spirit of power and love and self-discipline" (see also I Tim 4:14). Since Timothy in turn lays hands on others (I Tim 5:2), the gift of the Spirit is attached to commissioning, so that the Spirit enables the one commissioned to complete the assigned task. A Spirit thus attached to office can be mentioned infrequently since assumably, when the task is being done, the Spirit is at work.[96]

Pneuma is used 14 times in Ephesians, but only twice in Colossians! Most of the uses do not pertain directly to ecclesiology,[97] although once again there appears common Christian tradition about the reception of the Spirit at baptism ("sealing" in Eph 1:13; 4:30).

---

95. Non-ecclesiological uses include references to Christ's resurrection (I Tim 3:16) and to prophecy (I Tim 4:1).

96. Luke shows knowledge of apostles and of church offices in Acts, but he does not attach the Spirit to office. The most one can say is "In Acts the Spirit is given only when the Twelve are present or a member or delegate of the Twelve is on the scene," or that Luke has a vision of a "Spirit-guided organized church" (Fitzmyer, *Luke* [ftnote 92 above] 231,256—in the latter instance citing Käsemann).

97. The Spirit is mentioned in standard Christian wishes, formulas, and prayers (Col 1:8; 2:5; Eph 1:17; 2:18,22; 3:16; 4:3,23; 5:18; 6:17,18). Also mentioned are the Spirit in prophecy (Eph 3:5) and the evil spirit (Eph 2:2).

But the role of the Spirit in relation to the master concept of the church as the body of Christ is not clear. There is no mention of the Spirit in this connection in Colossians; and although Eph 4:4 writes of "one body and one Spirit," there is no explanation of the interrelation. The two letters are startlingly silent about the Spirit as the animating force of the body, for Christ the head has that role.[98] Christ and the Spirit are very close in NT thought; and where Christ is stressed as ongoing and active, often there is less emphasis on the activity of the Spirit.[99] The church of Colossians/Ephesians is not just on this earth; it reaches up into heaven which is the realm of the risen Christ.

In Luke/Acts, by contrast, Jesus Christ ascends to heaven while those who believe in him remain on earth. They are discouraged from looking longingly at the heavens (Acts 1:11), for the gift of the Spirit is precisely to take the place of Christ on earth.[100] The consequent massive importance attributed to the Spirit *in church history* is unique to Acts in the NT.[101] The author is not clear about whether he thinks of the Spirit as a person, but one cannot doubt the power of the Spirit. The crucial Pentecost scene is shaped by the imagery of the wind as the Spirit of God[102] moving over the face of the waters at

---

98. Good on this point are German articles on Christ and the Spirit in Ephesians (R. Schnackenburg) and in Colossians (E. Schweizer) in *Christ and Spirit in the New Testament*, ed. B. Lindars and S. S. Smalley (C.F.D. Moule Festschrift; Cambridge Univ. 1973) 279–96, 297–313. It is interesting to contrast II Cor 3:18, "We are being changed into the likeness of the Lord from one degree of glory to another, for this comes *from* the Lord who is *the Spirit*," and Col 2:19, "*the head from whom* the whole body, nourished and knit together, . . . grows with a growth that is from God."

99. C.F.D. Moule, "Jesus of Nazareth and the Church's Lord," in *Die Mitte des Neuen Testaments*, ed. U. Luz and H. Weder (E. Schweizer Festschrift; Göttingen: Vandenhoeck & Ruprecht, 1983) 176–86, is a fascinating treatment of this problem. Some contemporary distortions tend to translate the ongoing Jesus into the presence of the Spirit, so that Jesus becomes purely a past figure.

100. Luke is affected by the Synoptic Gospel format taken over from Mark where the description of Jesus' career is terminated by death and resurrection. In this way Luke parts from the Pauline heritage, for both the undisputed and post-Pauline Epistles are silent about the earthly ministry of Jesus before the crucifixion and resurrection.

101. I do not plan to discuss every aspect of the work of the Spirit in Acts but only the main ecclesial contributions. See E. Haenchen *The Acts of the Apostles* (Oxford: Blackwell, 1971) 92–93; and Fitzmyer, *Luke* [ftnote 92 above] 1.227–31.

102. Both in Hebrew and in Greek the same word can be used for "wind" and "spirit."

the creation (Gen 1:2), and by the imagery of the God of the storm coming down on Mount Sinai to make a covenant with Israel as His people (Exod 19:16ff.). In the last days a new creative act of God is taking place that matches the first creation; Jerusalem has replaced Sinai as the site of a renewed covenant[103] that will touch all peoples. And so there comes a sound resembling a mighty wind, while tongues of fire are distributed, filling with the Holy Spirit those who are to proclaim this renewed covenant (Acts 2:14–17).

Up to that moment after the resurrection, because they lacked either understanding or courage, the apostles had not proclaimed publicly what God had done in and through Jesus. The first step in making the following of Jesus a missionary movement is attributed by Acts to that Spirit with which the apostles were baptized and empowered to speak (Acts 1:5,8; 2:33; 4:8,31). Reception of the Spirit marked entry into the group of believers attracted by this preaching (2:38; 8:15–17; 9:17; 15:8; 19:5–6). The Spirit directed missionaries to promising areas (8:29,39). In particular, the Spirit directed Peter to the house of Cornelius and guided in detail the admission and baptism of the first Gentiles (10:38,44–47; 11:12,15). The Spirit gave the impetus for Barnabas and Paul to set out on a mission that would convert whole communities of Gentiles (13:2,4). A most important decision was made in early Christian history when Peter, Paul, and James agreed to admit Gentiles without requiring circumcision. It was phrased in these terms: "It has seemed good to the Holy Spirit and to us not to burden you" (15:28). The Spirit prevented Paul from taking a detour that would have delayed his planting Christianity in Europe (16:6–7). Paul's decision that he must go to Rome is a resolve in the Spirit (19:21); and when Paul bids farewell to Asia, the Holy Spirit has been provident by making presbyters who are overseers (bishops) of the flock (20:28). Thus every essential step in this story of how witness was borne to Christ from Jerusalem to the ends of the earth is guided by the Spirit, whose presence becomes obvious at great moments where the human agents would otherwise be hesitant or choose wrongly.

---

103. We know that in Jesus' time the feast of Weeks or Pentecost served to commemorate the giving of the covenant to Moses on Sinai. The Essenes who gave us the Dead Sea Scrolls chose this feast for admitting new members to their community of the new covenant.

STRENGTHS AND WEAKNESSES

I have concentrated on two dominant factors in the ecclesiology of Acts: on *continuity* from Israel through Jesus to Peter and to Paul, and on the *intervention of the Holy Spirit* at crucial moments. Both these factors would have been enormously helpful in enabling the church or churches that read Luke/Acts to survive, once the apostles had died. Indeed, as I noted, the deaths of Peter and of Paul did not even merit a mention by Luke. The culmination of Acts' story of Peter's career came when he confirmed Paul's circumcision-free ministry to the Gentiles (Acts 15); Paul made a farewell speech to the presbyter-bishops of Ephesus passing on the care of the flock to them since they would see him no more (Acts 20:25,28). The chain of continuity shows a meticulous plan of God leading toward the victory of Christianity over the whole earth. Individuals play an assigned role; but when they pass away after having played the role, to the eyes of faith they confirm that the plan will take care of the future as well as it has taken care of the past.

Luke has built into his sketch of a divinely prepared continuity some elements that could give Gentile Christians a sense of pride. In a world where many Greco-Romans despised religions from the East as superstitious sects, it was important for Christians to know that their religion had a distinguished pedigree. Luke goes out of his way to mention Roman emperors and governors in relation to the birth of Jesus and the beginning of his ministry (Luke 2:1–2; 3:1–2). Luke also stresses Roman officials in relation to Paul's travels, especially the journey to Rome which takes place because of Paul's appeal to the emperor (Acts 13:7; 18:12; 23:26; 25:1–2,12). Belief in Christ is a religion that touches the political figures of the great world, even if indirectly. It may have begun in Jerusalem, but God's plan led it to Rome; and the empire is its destiny. To have had a significant past helps to give confidence about the future; and Luke supplied Christianity with a history that gave it that confidence. If the Paul of Acts says that he is "a citizen of no mean city," the Christians who read Acts came away with a pride that they were adherents to no mean religion.

In reassuring the Lucan churches about survival, even more important would have been Acts' portrayal of a Holy Spirit that intervenes at crucial moments when even the leaders needed help. The idea that on their own the Christian leaders would not have known what steps to take were it not for the dramatic (and even intrusive) guidance of the Spirit relativizes the importance of the apostolic generation. Peter and Paul were great instruments of the Spirit, but other instruments can and will be provided. The Spirit that brought faith to the Gentiles and brought Paul to Rome continues and will help the church in moments of need. For Christian self-understanding, how important through the centuries has been the idea that the Holy Spirit will not let the church down! When Christians encountered error and stupidity that seemed to threaten survival, how often have they exclaimed, "Thank God there is a Holy Spirit to pull us through, despite church leadership." Again and again in church history, when something marvelously unexpected has happened, Christian faith has discovered there the Spirit guiding the church. Acts' magnificent insight that the Spirit was at work in church history has been an enduring legacy in Christian self-analysis ever since.

What then are the possible weaknesses of the Lucan contribution to eccelesiology? A triumphal picture is painted in Acts. All setbacks are temporary and quickly turn out for good[104] in a Christian movement that is constantly growing numerically (2:41; 4:4; 6:1,7; 8:12; 9:31; 21:19–20) and geographically (1:8). On finishing Acts, the reading audience might quite logically have concluded that very soon afterwards the whole world would become Christian, as stated confidently by Paul: "Let it be known to you that this salvation of God has been sent to the Gentiles; and they will listen" (28:28). The plan of continuity presented in Luke/Acts is oriented toward the bigger and better; it does not prepare for major defeats or for losses that are not recouped. Such an ecclesiology, taken in isolation, will leave Christians perplexed when their institutions begin to close, when their churches are being abandoned for lack of members, and when

---

104. Even the delay in the second coming serves to give "the men of Israel" a chance to convert (3:17–20). The only defeat that seems to be final is one prophesied by Isaiah: that Israel will never understand or perceive God's word about Jesus (28:25–26). Some modern scholars would ameliorate even that judgment by arguing that it is not harmonious with Luke's benevolent emphasis throughout the work (see ftnote 84 above). But at the start Luke 2:34 recorded a prophecy that Jesus would lead to the downfall of many in Israel.

their overall numbers in the world begin to get smaller. For instance, in America, Roman Catholicism prided itself on ever increasing numbers dutifully recorded each year in the national *Catholic Directory.* In the late 1970s as the increase began to falter, the question was frequently asked if the church was finished.

Indeed, throughout church history it is fascinating to see how often Christian failures have been explained away because of the principle that the church cannot fail. The loss to Islam of important Christian regions in North Africa and the Near East was accounted for by a type of divine balance sheet. While God was taking these areas away from the church, He was giving her Northern Europe where the missionaries were converting Germanic and Scandinavian tribes to Christianity. If God deprived the Roman Catholic Church of half of Europe through the Reformation, Catholics consoled themselves with the idea that He had given her an even larger number of Catholics in Central and South America. Protestants had their form of historical optimism: the American Colonies constituted a new Promised Land where the corrupt Christianity of Rome would not be tolerated and a pure, reformed Christianity would flourish. The Protestant missionary movement that swept out of America and England in the nineteenth century would ultimately lead to the triumph of Bible Christianity.

To us today, an element of historical manipulation is obvious in all these explanations and dreams; but consciously or unconsciously they were influenced by the program of world conversion sketched in Acts 1:8. The solution is not to reject Acts, despite the perennial temptation to improve the canon. Rather the fullness of the canon needs to be taken seriously if the triumphalism of Acts is not to become impossibly romantic at a time of numerically shrinking Christianity. The OT is also in the canon; and it narrates how God's people shrank from twelve tribes to one, how religious institutions failed (monarchy, priesthood, sacrificial cult), and how Israel learned more about God in the ashes of the Temple destroyed by the Babylonians than in the elegant period of that Temple under Solomon. Placing the long Deuteronomic history of the monarchy alongside the brief history of the Christian movement in Acts may warn Bible readers that God's message to His people is not an unconditioned promise of increasing numbers to the ends of the earth.

A similar danger of triumphalism surrounds the role of the intervening Spirit in Acts. It is essential to Christians that the Spirit does intervene in church history and crises, and that some major decisions have been reached with the help of the Spirit, often against the inclination of church leadership. But granting that, can we be sure that the Holy Spirit will always come to the rescue? Does not the picture in Acts lead easily to a *deus ex machina* concept of the Spirit? Has God really given a blank check so that in every major instance the Spirit will make sure that the church will muddle through? In Rev 3:20 Jesus says, "Here I am. I stand at the door and knock; I will enter and dine with anyone who hears my voice and opens the door." Is it not true that there have been times in church history when no one opened the door, and the opportunity to answer Christ did not come again?

Two examples will illustrate the strength and weakness of an ecclesiology in which intervention by the Spirit plays a major role. The first example involves the story of ecumenism in this century. It was a Protestant movement traceable in its early days to several organizations that fused to become the World Council of Churches. Various factors affected its growth: two great wars, the disintegrating effects of secularism, the needs of the missions, etc. Even the Orthodox churches began to show interest, and finally adamant Roman Catholic opposition was dramatically reversed at Vatican II. Consequently, in one decade, the 1970s, more was accomplished toward friendly dialogue between Christians of many churches than in the preceding 450 years since the Augsburg Confession. Christians are scarcely romantic when they detect here the work of the creator Spirit, giving the churches an opportunity they never expected and could not have planned. But are we then to assume that the Spirit will bring the work to a triumphal conclusion? If in the next two decades the churches do not seize the opportunity, if a union between two major churches does not take place as a sign of what may be possible, and if consequently Christianity enters the third millennium much more divided than it entered the second millennium,[105] is it not

---

105. It is worth remembering that in the year 1000, with the exception of the relatively small monophysitic churches of the East, Christianity was not divided. We have now spent a thousand years undoing Christian unity.

possible, and even likely, that the opportunity will never come again? Almost by definition the Spirit surprises, but at times the surprise may be that the Spirit lets God's people pay the price of its failures. Surely the OT story makes that suspicion likely.

A second example of the complexity of the role assigned to the Spirit can bring to a close our discussion of three different forms of ecclesiology in the Pauline heritage, for it involves all three. Vatican II constituted for Roman Catholics almost a parade example of different ecclesiologies in tension. Before the Council Rome sent out to the participants preliminary forms of the documents to be discussed. In particular, the Holy Office, of which the Pope himself was prefect, greatly influenced the shaping of the document that would deal with Scripture: The Two Sources of Revelation. This preliminary document was extremely negative toward modern theology and biblical research, documenting its warnings with references to the modernist heresy at the beginning of the century. In a sense one could regard this as an exercise of the ecclesiology of the Pastorals: presbyter-bishops teaching officially against false doctrine and "itching ears"—an ecclesiology wherein the teaching office is certified by the Spirit at the laying on of hands. A solemn invocation of the Holy Spirit opened the Council; for surely the Spirit would be expected to intervene in such a Council where decisions could have enormous impact on Catholics and, through them, on Protestants as well. This might be regarded as an exercise of the ecclesiology of Acts where the meeting or council in Jerusalem prefaced its decision: "It has seemed good to the Holy Spirit and to us" (15:28). As I mentioned in Chapter 3 above, the chief biblical image known to the Council Fathers and one that might be expected to guide strongly their discussion of the church was the image of the body of Christ, derived from the ecclesiology of Colossians/Ephesians.

What happened when all three ecclesiologies came into play at the Council? The Council Fathers rejected resoundingly the preliminary document submitted to them which reflected the official teaching of the Holy Office. Church teachers stood on the floor of the Council and challenged other church teachers about the very direction of the Scriptures. Spirit-endowed officers envisioned by the Pastorals were in disagreement with each other, and the on-rushing Spirit envisioned in Acts led the majority to correct the trend of the official teaching dominant in Rome before the Council. In the discussion, the Colossians/Ephesians imagery of the body of Christ gradually yielded to the imagery of the people of God in order to facilitate the self-reform of the spotless bride. In other words, the three post-Pauline ecclesiological elements functioned in tension.

After the Council in which the surprising intervention of the Spirit seemed to dominate, the reforms to be put into effect were entrusted to church administrators; and so the ecclesiology of the Pastorals came back into play in a major way. At times the reforms led to excesses, for some within the church exaggerated the changes, so that the end product of the Spirit's working at the Council was as surprising as the working itself. I predicted in Chapter 3 that eventually the Roman Catholic Church, tired of internal disorder and divisive self-criticism, would have to rediscover as prominent the image of the body of Christ in order to preserve the sense of a church holiness that comes from Christ and goes beyond the status of the members. This means that tension between the ecclesiological elements is shifting after the Council as befits the needs of the church. Only in such flux, I would contend, can the strengths and weaknesses in the ecclesiologies of the Pauline heritage come into play and work for the betterment of the church.

CHAPTER 5

The Petrine Heritage in I Peter: The Church as the People of God

AFTER DISCUSSING THE PAULINE HERITAGE, we turn to I Peter which has close relationships to Pauline thought.[106] Elsewhere I have explained why I agree with those scholars who hold that this letter was written from Rome by a Petrine disciple, probably about the 80s or 90s.[107] (Thus it may have been contemporary with some of the post-Pauline works we have been considering.) The significant parallels between I Peter and Paul's Epistle to the Romans may be explicable because there Paul was trying to make his theology acceptable to the Christian community at Rome. That church was strongly attached to its Jewish origins and was closer to the missionary enterprise of James and Peter than to the mission of Paul.[108]

106. These are widely recognized; but Koester, *Introduction to the New Testament* (Philadelphia: Fortress, 1982) 2.292, goes too far when he treats I Peter alongside the post-Paulines as part of the transformation of *Pauline* theology into ecclesiastical doctrine.

107. See Brown, *Antioch* 128–30. Balanced presentations of this thesis are given by E. Best, *I Peter* (New Century Bible; Greenwood, SC: Attic, 1971), and by J. H. Elliott, *A Home for the Homeless* (Philadelphia: Fortress, 1981) 270–95.

108. In *Antioch* 1–9, and in "Not Jewish Christianity and Gentile Christianity, but Types of Jewish/Gentile Christianity," CBQ 45 (1983) 74–79, I have made a case for positing at least four different types of Jewish-Christian missions to the Gentiles. Two of them would have been more conservative than Paul in having Gentile converts preserve aspects of Judaism. I associate James and Peter with a mission that did not insist on circumcision but did insist on an observance of some Jewish customs and cultic features.

Since Romans is more temperate about the benefits of Judaism than some of the earlier Pauline letters, it may have won Paul acceptance in the church of the capital of the empire; and his martyrdom there would have hallowed his memory. By the end of the century, in a letter of the Roman church to Corinth (*I Clement* 5:2-5), Peter and Paul have become church pillars. That very ordering or sequence of names, with Peter first, is consistent in the early Rome-related documents of church history; it indicates that the Pauline heritage is now filtered through the prism of Petrine Christianity. The main thrust of the ecclesiology of I Peter is different from the thrusts of the three post-Pauline ecclesiologies we have discussed in earlier chapters because of its insistent description of the church against the background of Israel—a difference consistent with the picture of Roman Christianity I have drawn.

I Peter (1:1) is addressed "To the chosen exiles of the diaspora in Pontus, Galatia, Cappadocia, Asia, and Bithynia." From the contents of the letter the addressees are Gentile converts to Christianity, with a hint that the conversion had taken place some years previously. The exact area in Asia Minor in which they lived is not clear because we do not know whether the names refer to regions or provinces, but it is likely that most of the area was north of the limits of Paul's mission. Three of the five names (Cappadocia, Pontus, and Asia) are found in the list in Acts 2:9, a list that may describe the spread of Jerusalem Christianity; and so the area could have been evangelized by missionaries loyal to James and Peter. (Paul resisted building on another man's foundation. Did the Holy Spirit forbid Paul to preach in Asia and Bithynia [Acts 16:6-7] because Jerusalem missionaries were already there?) This would explain why the area is addressed in Peter's name from Rome, for plausibly Peter was more closely associated with the *Gentile* thrust of the Jerusalem mission.[109] Rome, the site of Peter's death, seemingly looked on itself as responsible for the ongoing care of that mission.[110]

---

109. The Epistle associated with James (1:1) is addressed "To the *twelve tribes* in the diaspora," an address suggesting that the name of James was associated with the Jerusalem mission to the *Jews* outside Palestine (also Acts 21:20).

110. Ignatius (Introduction to *Romans*) speaks of the preeminence in love of the Roman church; and in *Romans* 3:1 he comments that the Roman church taught others. Evidently, the church of Rome felt free to send *I Clement* to admonish the church

What were the Gentiles of northern Asia Minor told by this letter from Rome? The first chapter offers by way of reminder a fundamental way of looking at Christian conversion and at the status of Christian life.[111] This presentation of *Christian basics* is heavily influenced by the OT, for the exodus, desert wandering, and promised land motifs from the Pentateuch have been taken over and imaginatively reapplied to the conversion of Gentiles to Christ. If that desert experience made the slave tribes from Egypt into a people, nay God's people, so has Christian conversion made the Gentiles who were once no people into God's people.

Let me illustrate this from the text of I Peter. If the Hebrews who left Egypt were told to gird up their loins for quick departure (Exod 12:11), the Gentile Christian recipients of I Peter are told to gird up the loins of their mind (1:13). If in the desert the Israelites murmured and wanted to go back to the fleshpots of Egypt (Exod 16:2–3), the recipients of I Peter are warned about the longings of their former ignorance (1:14). Moses was ordered to tell the people whom God was making His own, "Be holy, for I, the Lord your God, am holy" (Lev 19:2); the same charge is quoted to the recipients of I Peter (1:15–16). Christian life is described as a time of exile or sojourning with the hope of an inheritance yet to be attained (I Peter 1:17; 1:4), echoing Israel's desert wandering before it reached its inheritance in the promised land. Redemption and even the paying of a ransom were figures of speech used to describe God's liberation of His people from Egypt (Exod 6:5–6; Deut 7:8; Isa 52:3), and so it is not surprising to find in I Peter 1:18: "You know that you were ransomed from the empty ways handed down from your fathers." The Israelites fashioned a calf and worshiped it as the god who brought them out of the land of Egypt (Exod 32:1–4), a calf made with the silver and gold the Hebrew women got from their Egyptian neighbors at the time of the tenth plague (11:2). Yet, in fact, the Hebrews had been spared from that plague by the blood of

---

of Corinth (where there was a group of Peter's adherents during Paul's lifetime); and Dionysius of Corinth mentions another early letter from Rome to Corinth (Eusebius, *Hist.* 4.23.10–11).

111. We need not enter the long debates about whether chap. 1 of I Peter (and part of chap. 2) represents in whole or in part a baptismal homily, a baptismal liturgy, a baptismal hymn, or a baptismal confession.

the unblemished passover lamb marking their houses (12:5–7). The echoes of this appear in the continuation of I Peter 1:18–19: ". . . ransomed not with perishable things such as silver and gold, but with the precious blood of Christ, as of a lamb without blemish or spot."

The imagery drawn from the story of Israel continues into the second chapter of I Peter, especially imagery dealing with cult. Working with the metaphor of Christ as a stone, the author challenges his audience: "You yourselves, like living stones, are being built into a spiritual house to be a holy priesthood, to offer spiritual sacrifices to God through Jesus Christ" (2:5). Later he makes clear that in part these spiritual sacrifices consist of good conduct that will bear witness to the pagans (2:12). In evaluating such language, one should note that I Peter betrays knowledge of church structure similar to that envisioned by the Pauline Pastorals, for in 5:1 Peter is a presbyter speaking to fellow presbyters about their supervision of the flock. Yet there is no resort to presbyteral structure to encourage the audience who are undergoing a fiery trial (4:12). Why is Israelite imagery centered on the people of God so important as a response to the need of Gentile Christians?

STRENGTHS AND WEAKNESSES

The answer to that question is facilitated by a reconstruction of the situation in which the addressees found themselves. Much has been written assuming that they were facing a full-scale Roman persecution (under Nero, or Domitian, or Trajan). But recently J. H. Elliott and others have been persuasive in their contention that the real issue was alienation and ostraciscm. In the "backwoods" area of northern Asia Minor those who had become Christians felt themselves cut off from the surrounding society. In the eyes of their pagan neighbors they were a curious and secretive sect.[112] Later Roman evidence includes charges of atheism, for Christians did not worship the

---

112. Besides building up the self-confidence of his readers, the author is careful to warn them not to give pagan Gentiles any objective reasons to hate them. They are to maintain good conduct among the Gentiles so that the charges of wrongdoing will not be justified (2:12); they are to be subject obediently to the emperor as supreme and

civic gods, and charges of anti-social behavior, for they had closed meals and meetings. Inevitably there was the danger that converts, feeling this contempt, might go back to "the passions of their former ignorance" (1:14).[113]

I Peter counteracted this alienation by the assurance that in Christianity Gentile converts had found a new family, a new home, a new status that made them a special people with an imperishable inheritance. All the pride of the Israelites as the special people of God was now being transferred to Gentiles who had "tasted the kindness of the Lord" (2:3). Inculcating this proud sense of belonging was a difficult task. Jews, after all, had a certain blood relationship, since by definition a Jew is one born of a Jewish mother; but hitherto these Gentiles of diverse stock who had converted to Christ had little in common. "Once you were no people, but now you are the people of God; once you had not received (God's) gracious mercy, but now you have received that mercy" (2:10). In other words, in their Christian status converts were being told that they had found something better: "You are a chosen race, a royal priesthood, a holy nation, God's own people" (2:9).

The strength of the ecclesiology proclaimed by I Peter rests in the sense that real benefits are gained from belonging. If people feel that they get something worthwhile from being members of a church, that church will survive. The people of God in the OT, Israel, went on as God's people after Moses and Joshua disappeared from the scene; the people of God in the NT, the church, will go on after Peter and the other apostles have disappeared from the scene. The more poorly defined the family or social context from which new members come into a community, the more deeply they will be attracted by encountering a loving care that gives them a new identity or dignity. Today we see this verified in the attraction that religious sects or various types of charismatic communities have for

---

to governors who exercise a legitimate power of punishing (2:13–14); they are not to use their Christian freedom as a pretext for evil but are to silence the ignorance of foolish men (2:15–16); if they are to love in a special way the inner family of Christians (the brotherhood), they are to honor all (2:17).

113. Those passions are condemned in 4:2ff., and dismissed with a phrase that betrays the author's (and the Roman church's) background in Judaism: "Doing what the Gentiles like to do."

those who are unhappy with their family, their church, the civil order, or the world in general. This attraction constitutes a special
challenge to traditional churches where Sunday attendance has been
a matter of obligation or societal expectation. Obligation and expectation are often no longer strong enough in themselves to insure
church attendance; and so unless people have a sense of benefit
gained from attendance, they will go to a group that gives that sense.

Similarly imperiled are large parishes where communicants
scarcely know each other and have no sense of family closeness or
sense of the church as their home. Means must be found for breaking
these parishes down into smaller groups that give identity to the
alienated. In former times, in rural or agrarian sections of the country, the church or chapel to which one belonged was the center of
one's life. Within my own tradition, to give a contemporary example,
it is fascinating to see the attractiveness of "homey" Newman centers
on university campuses, drawing Roman Catholic students who
would not voluntarily cross the threshhold of their parish churches.
The centers often offer lively participation in liturgies, peer friendship, and a wholesome social life to a very alienated age-bracket.
Such examples may help us to understand how the author of I Peter
thought that membership in a Christian house church, when properly understood, could make a community (people) out of converts os-
tracized by their families and friends, and who consequently felt lost
or alone in many aspects of their lives.

The dignity of "royal priesthood, holy nation" mentioned in I
Peter highlights a particular problem today for Christian churches
that speak of an ordained priesthood. Precisely because much of
Protestantism ceased to designate Christian ministry as priesthood
(on the grounds of biblical silence[114]), Roman Catholic theology but-
tressed the ordained priesthood. It was emphasized that the one ordained to the priesthood was metaphysically changed and indelibly
marked by the sacrament; even Vatican II insisted that the difference
of the ordained from the non-ordained was one of kind and not simply of degree. Consequently little emphasis was placed in Catholi-

---

114. Nowhere in the NT are church presbyters or bishops called priests; that development came for bishops in the second century, and later for presbyters. It is interesting that I Peter speaks of a general "royal priesthood" (2:9) and of "presbyters"
(5:1) but makes no connection between them.

cism on the priesthood of believers. I believe we Roman Catholics need to recover for our people I Peter's sense of priestly dignity and spiritual sacrifices, precisely as a way of underlining the status conferred on all Christians.[115] Similarly, holiness has been too emphatically associated with special forms of Catholic life, e.g., religious vocation and the observance of vows. The unique status of holiness given by baptism to all believers needs to be stressed.

If the strengths of I Peter's ecclesiology lie in the sense of a belonging to a close-knit unique group and the consequent acquisition of identity and dignity, what are the weaknesses? The chief problem is the sense of exclusive eliteness inherent in designating any group as belonging more closely to God. If a consciousness of being the unique people of God has enabled Israel and the Jews to survive over 3000 years of world history, it also explains some of the dislike and hatred directed toward Jews. Similarly, while the belief that they were bringing pagans into the special people of God sparked Christian missionaries from the first century down to the twentieth century, often the rest of the populace in a country invaded by missionaries have felt umbrage at being told explicitly or implicitly that they were not the people of God and thus being relegated to a lesser theological status. If the Christian converts of northern Asia Minor needed to have I Peter reemphasize their special status as a support against ostracism and contempt by their pagan compatriots, we can be sure that a strengthened sense of status led inevitably to even more hatred of Christians by pagans.

The Jewish and Christian self-justification of the "people of God" concept is that the unique dignity is conferred by God's graciousness and does not imply special worthiness on the part of the recipients. This explanation based on God's sovereign freedom of choice is helpful, but we must recognize that in an increasingly pluralistic society the exclusiveness inherent in the concept is bound to

---

115. Other Catholics fear that such emphasis will imperil the unique status of the ordained priesthood. Human nature being what it is, an emphasis on either side imperils existentially the truth on the other side, even if one states that that other truth should not be overlooked. As for which priesthood needs shoring, I see ordained priests marked off by many visual signs (clerical dress, vestments, celibate life), while most Catholic laity are completely ignorant that the term priesthood is applicable to them.

be resented by outsiders and embarrassing to many insiders. It is an aspect of the "outside of the church there is no salvation" problem. Whatever that statement may have meant originally, most Christians feel instinctively that it cannot be true that only Christians are saved.[116] Yet there remains an authentic Christian belief that God saves through Jesus Christ—indeed, saves also those who do not believe in Jesus Christ—and so a relationship, even if unconscious, to the church of Christ is involved in salvation. We Christians have never developed a satisfactory way of reconciling God's unique gift of grace through Christ and God's merciful love for all.

Let me add two troublesome corollaries of the exclusiveness inherent in the "people of God" concept. With sovereign assurance I Peter writes to the Gentile Christians, "You are God's own people," without mentioning that another group had a prior claim to that title, namely, the Jews. I pointed out above that the whole imagery of the exodus, desert wandering, paschal lamb, and promised land are taken over and used to interpret the pilgrimage involved in coming to faith in Christ; but there is no indication that historically these happenings and symbols pertained to a people existing long before Jesus. Perhaps the author believed that through faith in Christ the Gentiles were being joined to the existing people of God, Israel, and thus were able to appropriate Israelite symbolism. (That would be close to the theology of Eph 2:11–22 which shares much Israelite symbolism with I Peter 1:13 – 2:10—a sharing that suggests that we are reading standard baptismal terminology. In Ephesians the Gentiles who were alienated from the commonwealth of Israel have in

---

116. Of course, there are some who do believe that only Christians (or indeed one species of Christians) are saved. Often they cite John 3:5: "Unless a person is born of water and the Spirit, that person cannot enter the kingdom of heaven" (with the implication, probably correct, that this birth refers to baptism). They call attention to the universal negative involved in "unless" and insist that this is the word of God settling the issue. Unfortunately, they feel no need to ask what was in the author's mind when he wrote these words, for they do not recognize that every word written in Scripture is humanly conditioned. The Johannine writer was denying the Jewish understanding that one becomes part of the people of God by natural birth from a Jewish mother. In his theology only begetting or birth from God produces a child of God, and what is born of the flesh is flesh. He was not dealing with the issue of people who did their best to serve God but had never found Christ proclaimed convincingly enough (especially by example) to warrant belief. It is not obvious, then, how the Johannine statement affects the latter situation.

Christ Jesus been brought near and the two made one.) But I Peter never mentions Israel or the Jews or the joining of the two into one. It is as if there is and has been no previous claimant to the title [117] other than the Christians! Following out this implication but going beyond it, by the next century Christians would be explicitly denying that the Jews were still the people of God, for they had been replaced by Christians. Today some Christians would revoke that step by arguing that there are two peoples of God or two groups within the one people of God: His children of Israel and His children through Christ. But other Christians adamantly refuse to allow the title "people of God" to the Jews,[118] and I rather doubt that there are many Jews who are willing to share the precise title with Christians. Such is the exclusiveness inherent in the concept.

Still another corollary that I mention briefly is that in I Peter's ecclesiology the status of holiness has been acquired by coming to Christ or into the church. The outsiders (Gentiles who have not been converted) will see Christians and glorify God at the judgment (2:12). There is no reference to the existence of holiness in outsiders or to reaching out to the non-Christians with any appreciation of the goodness they already have. In Vatican II, the document "On the Church in the Modern World" called for a Christian appreciation of the possibilities and structures of the surrounding world, even if they are non-Christian. Strangely enough that call came at a time when the "people of God" imagery was being adopted massively. Perhaps the combination occurred because the positive side of the imagery appealed pastorally (as it did to the author of I Peter) by emphasizing the status of being a Christian, and the negative side of the imagery was overlooked. Or perhaps the language of "people" was thought to create a bond between Christians and others in this world. Yet biblically the status of the people of God reduces all others to being a non-people.[119]

---

117. The statement, "Once you were no people," addressed to Gentiles, echoes a Jewish outlook, but does not explicitly deal with the status of the Jews.

118. Indeed, there are Christian groups that would carry the exclusivity farther by denying that other *Christian* groups deserve the title.

119. Similarly, for NT authors like John and Paul only believers are children of God.

CHAPTER 6

The Heritage of the Beloved Disciple
in the Fourth Gospel:
A Community of People Personally Attached
to Jesus

T HE CONCEPT of the body of Christ in the Colossians/Ephesians
segment of the post-Pauline heritage and the concept of the people of God in the post-Petrine heritage, while quite distinct, have in
common a strong sense of ecclesial *collectivity*. We now come to another heritage, the Johannine heritage or, more precisely, that of the
Beloved Disciple, as attested in the Gospel and Epistles of John.[120]
The ecclesiology of this heritage is distinguished by its emphasis on
the relation of the individual Christian to Jesus Christ. I do not mean
that John anticipates the individualism of American frontier preaching, embodied in the slogan "Jesus is my personal savior," which

---

120. The Gospel purports to report the witness of the Disciple whom Jesus loved
(John 19:35; 21:24), and seemingly to have been written by that Disciple (21:24),
whom it never identifies by name. In the first volume of my Anchor Bible commentary (1966) I gave partial acceptance to the second-century identification of him as
John, son of Zebedee, by positing that perhaps John was the source of the tradition
but that the writer of the Gospel was an unknown. After another decade of research
for *Community* (1979) and my *Epistles* (1982) I was convinced that the identity of the
Disciple and that of the evangelist are unknown to us, for it is quite unlikely that the
Disciple was one of the Twelve. The German commentator on John, Rudolf Schnackenburg, independently went through the same change of mind (see ftnote 4 above).

somehow passes as biblical! The OT and Jewish roots of John (and of the NT in general) are too strong for that—in Christ God saved *a people*. That the fourth evangelist thought collectively is shown by the vine and branches symbolism of chap. 15 and by the shepherd and flock symbolism of chap. 10. Nevertheless, within this collective presupposition, there is an unparalleled concentration on the relation of the individual believer to Jesus. Another aspect of Johannine ecclesiology is the dwelling of the Paraclete-Spirit in the believer, and this aspect carries over into the Epistles of John. Although this second aspect is related to the first, I judge it more convenient to divide my treatment of the two aspects into separate chapters.

Ecclesiology in the Fourth Gospel is dominated by the extraordinary Johannine christology. Because we tend to blend together gospel pictures of Jesus, it is hard for us to realize that among the four gospels only John posits *explicitly* a pre-existent career of God's Son. Indeed, to some extent John's picture of Jesus is unique among NT writings. In the Pauline writings there are verses that have been interpreted as referring to pre-existence, but most of them are unclear or debatable. Even when one accepts the pre-existence interpretation, as I am willing to do for some passages, the Pauline references are poetic and none of them deals explicitly with a pre-existence *before creation*.[121] (The same cautions are true about the relatively clear pre-existence motif in Heb 1:2–3.) Pre-existence before creation appears poetically in John 1:1–3, but also in prose as a claim by Jesus himself in 17:5 (see 8:58). The Johannine Jesus had glory with his Father before the world began. He came down from heaven to this earth, became flesh, and revealed to people what he had seen and heard when he was with the Father. In *Community* I discussed in detail what may have contributed to the development of the profound Johannine insight into Jesus' wisdom and power;[122] and at the beginning of the next chapter I shall present, very briefly, a reconstructed

---

121. The most frequently cited Pauline allusions to pre-existence are I Cor 8:6; II Cor 8:9; Philip 2:6–7; Col 1:15–17; and I Tim 3:16. In my judgment the clearest Pauline passage is Col 1:15–17, and there the Son is the "firstborn of all creation."

122. Although the other gospels do not explicitly picture Jesus as pre-existent before creation, each gospel with its own nuance treats him as God's Son. Pre-existence is the Johannine explanation of the divine wisdom and power that all the gospels attribute to Jesus. The fact that in the later teaching pre-existence became the only orthodox explanation does not mean it was the only explanation in NT times.

history of the Johannine community.[123] Here, however, let me summarize the christology itself as a basis for the ecclesiology that developed from it.

A common picture in the early church was that, after an earthly ministry terminating in crucifixion and resurrection, Jesus went to the right hand of his Father until finally he would come down to earth in glory to exercise judgment. Without denying a final coming, John has radically transformed the gospel picture by insisting that Jesus already came down to earth from heaven in glory, so that his public ministry constituted judgment: "This is the judgment: the light has come into the world, but people preferred darkness to light" (John 3:19). Hitherto no one had seen God (1:18); but since Jesus has come from God, whoever has seen Jesus has seen the Father (14:9). Indeed, because as Son he has life from the Father, he can give us God's own life (6:57).[124] The basic thought is so simple that it is breathtaking. A child gets life from a parent, and the only life that our natural parents can give us is the life of the flesh (3:6). But if God begets us, we are God's children with His eternal life. That begetting comes through water and Spirit to those who believe in Jesus (1:12–13; 3:3–6).

Christians come into being through faith in Jesus, and they must continue attached to him in order to stay alive. Near the end of the first century, NT writers were picturing Jesus as the builder, founder, or cornerstone of the church (Matt 16:18; Eph 2:20). That imagery contains an important insight, but it suffers from some of the limitations of constructional language. The builder of a standing edifice did his work in the past; he is present only as a memory. A cornerstone is necessary in the construction if the building is going to stand; but it is inert, and no one thinks much about its presence once

---

123. In the third Sprunt Lecture I spelled out in detail what I abbreviate in these chapters; but that was because the Lectures came less than a year after the appearance of *Community* (Spring 1979), and the audience might not have been familiar with my approach to Johannine christology. Now there has been a wide circulation of *Community*, and it is available to those who want detail.

124. For John, Jesus *is God's Son*, while we *become God's children*. Neither the verb nor the noun seems to be interchangeable. Also we are begotten by God, and no passage says clearly that Jesus was begotten by God (despite the variant reading of John 1:13 with a singular subject; a disputed interpretation of I John 5:18; and a tendency to translate *monogenēs* as "only begotten" instead of literally as "only").

the building is dedicated. In other words, construction imagery can lead to relating Jesus to the church as one who is past or as an inert presence. John avoids all such imagery. Jesus is the vine, and Christians are branches getting life from the vine. More than the founder of the community, Jesus is the animating principle, still "alive and well" in its midst. He is the shepherd who tends the sheep that belong to him, knowing them and calling each by name. For eternal life one must continue to follow the shepherd or adhere to the vine (John 10:27–28; 15:2–6). This is an ecclesiology peculiarly shaped by christology. Within the collective imagery of vine and flock, the core of the ecclesiology is a personal, ongoing relation to the life-giver come down from God.

Let me illustrate the uniqueness of this ecclesiology by another example. The Jesus of the Synoptic Gospels introduces and proclaims God's kingdom, rule, or reign in the world. Much parabolic symbolism is applied to this heavenly rule: the rule/kingdom of God/heaven is like the sower or seed (Matt 13:3,11,24,31), a treasure or pearl (13:44,45), a fishnet (13:47), a vineyard (21:28,31,33,43), a royal wedding banquet (22:2). But in John, except for 3:3,5, "the kingdom/rule of God" is absent.[125] Rather the figurative or allegorical imagery is applied to Jesus himself, e.g., he is the bridegroom (John 3:29). Most frequently the metaphors are the predicate of his sovereign "I am": I am the vine (15:1,5); I am the sheepgate or the shepherd (10:7,9,11,14); I am the bread of life come down from heaven (6:35,41,51); I am the light of the world (8:12; 9:5). Why the shift from "the rule/kingdom of God is like" to "I am" as the subject of such imagery? One must guess, but the shift of meaning in *basileia* from "rule," implying an activity, to "kingdom," implying a place, may have been part of the motive. Above (p. 51), I pointed out that *basileia* not only was localized and reified, but (as the kingdom of the Son) was identified implicitly with the church. The absence of "kingdom" terminology in John prevents such a development. If Jesus and the Father are one, the rule of God is most perfectly made a reality in Jesus. Instead of entering the kingdom of God as a place, one needs to inhere in Jesus to be part of the community.

A similar history may be detected with regard to "sacra-

---

125. John 18:36 has Jesus speaking of "my kingdom" which is not of this world.

ments."[126] In Matt 28:19 the risen Jesus orders the eleven disciples:
"Go, make disciples of all nations, baptizing them in the name of the
Father and of the Son and of the Holy Spirit." In two of the four NT
eucharistic accounts, Jesus gives the order in reference to his body
and blood, "Do this in memory of me" (I Cor 11:25; Luke 22:19).
Such directives have led to the theological affirmation that Jesus instituted the sacraments. Valid as that is, once more we have the image of a founder—Jesus about to depart tells his disciples to do
things that he did not normally do, for nowhere in the Synoptic tradition does he baptize[127] and only at the last meal of his life does he
speak about bread and wine as his body and blood. Thus there is a
dichotomy: Jesus healed and preached, but the church baptizes and
celebrates the eucharist. (Often this results in complaints by clergy in
the more liturgical churches that their ministry is too involved with
sacraments and not enough with helping people in the way Jesus
did.)

John avoids the whole problem in two ways. First, the Fourth
Gospel has no institutional commands in regard to baptism and the
eucharist. Indeed, there is no eucharist at the Last Supper but only
the washing of the feet.[128] Second, Johannine sacramental references

---

126. The language of "sacraments" is not found in the NT, and we do not know
whether these first-century Christians brought baptism and the eucharist (and perhaps
other sacred actions) together under one rubric.

127. John 3:22 is the only gospel support for Jesus' having baptized, but that is
denied in 4:1–2. Perhaps Christians feared that to portray Jesus as a baptizer would
place him on the same level as John the Baptist, or even on a lower level since John
would have been the inaugurator of a baptizing ministry and Jesus would have been
the follower.

128. The substitution is scarcely accidental, even if the purpose is not totally
clear. (The tradition that Jesus spoke of his body and blood the night before he died is
too entrenched in Paul and the Synoptics for John to have been ignorant of it.) The
washing of the feet has similarities to the eucharist: same place in the meal, an action
symbolic of Jesus' self-giving in death, an accompanying command to repeat (John
13:15: "You shall do as I have done for you"). But the washing shows more clearly
than does the eucharist the theme of humble service by the Christian. Because it is so
sacred, the eucharist has been very divisive in Christian history with almost every aspect having been fought about. Would Christians have argued with each other so
fiercely over the washing of the feet? Many Christians vie for the privilege of presiding
at the eucharist. How many would vie for the "privilege" of washing another person's
dirty feet?

are made in relation to what Jesus normally did in his lifetime.[129] For instance, the most direct eucharistic reference, with an allusion to eating Jesus' flesh[130] and drinking his blood (6:51–58), is in commentary on the multiplication of the loaves, one of the rare events in the Galilean ministry that all four gospels agree on. The other gospels have no eucharistic aftermath of the multiplication; but for John, just as Jesus fed people in his lifetime with multiplied physical bread as a sign of the food that endures for eternal life (6:27), so he feeds them (through bread and wine) with his flesh and blood which are the food of eternal life. Other NT authors speak of the eucharist as a memorial of Jesus in which is proclaimed the death of the Lord until he comes; but John stresses the eucharist as food.[131] In the dialogue with Nicodemus (3:3–6) Jesus explains that eternal life is given through begetting/birth with water and Spirit; in the dialogue with the Jews after the multiplication Jesus explains that this eternal life is fed through his flesh and blood. This is the "real" or "true" life, birth, and food of which physical life, birth, and food are at most signs.[132] Let me give another example. "Enlightenment" was early Christian language for the process of conversion and entrance into the Christian community (Heb 6:4; 10:32; II Cor 4:6). John 9 gives us a story of how Jesus, the light of the world, gave physical sight to a man born blind, a story which becomes virtually a parable of how

---

129. The extent of sacramental allusions in John is strenuously debated; see Brown, *John* 1.CXI–CXIV.

130. The Johannine *sarx*, "flesh" (also used for the eucharist by Ignatius of Antioch), may be a more literal Greek rendition of the earliest Semitic eucharist formula. The three Synoptics and Paul use *sōma*, "body," which is more appropriate Greek; but in the Hebrew and Aramaic clearly datable to the time before or contemporary with Jesus, there is no word for "body." The word *gûph*, which later came to be used for "body," is attested only for "corpse" at that period. The normal Semitic formula for the human components is "flesh and blood."

131. Different eucharistic emphases in the NT are, at times unconsciously, at the root of different church practices today. When the eucharist (designated as the Lord's Supper) is presented as a memorial of what Jesus did on the night before he died, the dynamism of the theology points toward infrequent eucharists—Passover, after all, is a somewhat comparable Jewish memorial of a meal eaten the night before the departure from Egypt, and it occurs only once a year. But when the food aspect of the eucharist is stressed, there is clearly a dynamism toward frequent eucharist.

132. The basic Roman Catholic theology of sacraments as signs instituted by Christ echoes the Johannine understanding of signs.

spiritual sight was gained when the man came to faith in Jesus after being put on trial by the Jewish authorities.

In chaps. 6 and 9, then, Johannine readers were told of a Jesus who during his lifetime fed the hungry and gave sight to the blind by marvelous deeds that were, in turn, signs of a heavenly reality. At the same time, by the inclusion of ecclesiastical, sacramental language in these chapters, the Johannine writer was teaching that Jesus continues to give the enlightenment of faith and the food of eternal life through the signs of baptism and the eucharist. Jesus is not simply the one who instituted the sacraments of the church; he is the life-giver who remains active in and through those sacraments. Thus, the unique importance that John places on the relationship of the Christian to Jesus is being underlined through sacramental imagery.

This relationship to Jesus outweighs in importance all distinctions flowing from special service in the church. On this point one may contrast the Johannine imagery of the vine with the Pauline imagery of the body. In I Cor 12 Paul used the body imagery as a theological basis for rejecting jealousies about charisms. All the parts or members of the body are indispensable; and so there is no reason for the foot to be jealous of the hand, nor the ear jealous of the eye. "If the whole body were an eye, where would the sense of hearing be? If the whole body were an ear, where would the sense of smell be? But, as it is, God has arranged the members in the body, each one of them, just as He wanted them to be. If altogether there were only one member, where would the body be? As it is there are many members, yet one body" (I Cor 12:17–20). Similarly, there is no reason for those who have one charism (apostles, prophets, teachers, workers of miracles, healers, speakers in tongues) to desire another. It would not help if all were apostles, if all were prophets, etc.; for the church needs the diversity of members. The Johannine vine also is an image capable of such an interpretation. Stalk, branches, stems, leaves, and fruit could have been used to illustrate diverse charisms of service as easily as were the members of the body. But John writes only about the vine (Jesus) and the branches (Christians). The gospel shows no interest in diverse charisms that distinguish Christians: it is interested in a basic, life-receiving status enjoyed by all.

Were there diverse charisms within the Johannine community? As for prophets and teachers, only false prophets are mentioned (I

John 4:1), and the need for teachers is denied (I John 2:27).[133] A lack of distinction based on charisms or offices is especially noticeable in Johannine ecclesiology in the question of apostles. In the rest of the NT the importance of the apostle is clear. In the 30s till the mid-60s, i.e., the era in which the well-known apostles were alive and active, we find Paul's constant insistence on his own apostolate (Gal 1:1; I Cor 15:9–10; II Cor 11:5). He lists apostolate first among the charisms that God has established in the church (I Cor 12:28; see also Eph 2:20; 4:11). In the last one-third of the first century after the well-known apostles were dead, they are remembered prominently in the Synoptic Gospels, Acts, the post-Pauline and post-Petrine writings, and Revelation.[134] But the term "apostle" is completely absent from the Johannine writings—both from the gospel and (even more startlingly) from the three epistles.[135] No named apostle is exalted as the great hero of this community as was the case in the Pauline and Petrine heritages. Rather, the figure par excellence is a disciple, "the Disciple whom Jesus loved." I do not mean that the Johannine evangelist wished to deny the existence of apostles in Christian history. He mentions the Twelve (John 6:67,70,71; 20:24), and he could scarcely not have known that they were considered apostles. He knows of a sending forth (*apostellein*, 17:18) by Jesus, which is the basis of apostleship. But evidently apostleship is not what constitutes prime dignity in Johannine ecclesiology. The Fourth Gospel emphasizes *discipleship*, a status that all Christians enjoy; and within that status what confers dignity is the love of Jesus.

The difference between Johannine ecclesiology and that of other NT writers on this point is illustrated by the continual contrast between John's Beloved Disciple and Peter, the most prominent of the

---

133. Revelation (Apocalypse) is probably distantly related to the Johannine writings. Yet in attributing OT cultic dignity to the Christian people, Revelation is closer to I Peter than to John: Jesus Christ "who made us to be a kingdom and priests to serve his God and Father" (Rev 1:6; 5:10). There are references to apostles and (Christian) prophets in Revelation—figures missing in John.

134. There is no reference to apostles in James, Hebrews, and Philemon. Hebrews 3:1 speaks of Jesus as an apostle.

135. The word *apostolos* occurs in John 13:16: "No slave is greater than his master, no *messenger* is greater than the one who sent him." Although the meaning "messenger" is clear there, if one wanted to insist on using the translation "apostle" in that verse, the import would scarcely be favorable to a high image of apostles.

Twelve and (at least by the end of the century) the most prominent
apostle for the majority of Christians. In Matthew (16:16; 17:24;
18:21) Peter among the Twelve is the spokesman in addressing Jesus;
but at the Last Supper in John 13:22–26 Simon Peter cannot speak
directly to Jesus, for he is at a distance from him. Rather Peter must
speak to Jesus through the intermediary of the Beloved Disciple who
is closest to Jesus, reclining on Jesus' breast. In the Synoptic tradition Peter is the only one of the Twelve to follow the arrested Jesus
into the court or palace of the high priest. In John 18:15–16 Simon
Peter cannot follow Jesus into the courtyard until the Disciple ar-
ranges for admittance. In the Synoptic tradition even Peter ultimately abandons Jesus, so that no follower of Jesus stands close by as he
dies on the cross. In John one male follower never abandons Jesus,
for at the foot of the cross stands the Beloved Disciple, as well as the
mother of Jesus.[136] Indeed, by making his mother the mother of the
Beloved Disciple (19:26–27), Jesus is adopting this Disciple as his
brother. Thus, the scene at the cross supplies the Johannine answer
to the traditional question, "Who are my mother and my brothers?"[137]

Peter's prominent position in the church at large was heavily influenced by the remembrance in various NT circles that he was the
first among the Twelve to see the risen Jesus (I Cor 15:5; Luke
24:34). In John 20:8, however, when Simon Peter and the Beloved
Disciple run and look into the empty tomb, the Disciple (alone) believes without seeing the risen Jesus. Thus, while traditionally Peter
may have been the first apostle to see the risen Jesus, Johannine tradition knows of a Disciple who was even more blessed for having believed without such seeing. And even when these two men together
do see the risen Jesus, Simon Peter does not recognize the Lord until
the Disciple tells Peter it is the Lord (21:7). Love has brought the
Disciple closer to Jesus than was the most important apostle and
made him more perceptive. And if martyrdom at Rome made Peter a
pillar of the church (*I Clem.* 5:2–4), Jesus took special care of the
Disciple who was not a martyr (21:18–23); and he became the ongo-

---

136. One, two, or three other women stand there, depending on how one divides
the description in 19:25.

137. See Mark 3:33, and R. E. Brown, *et al., Mary in the New Testament* (New
York: Paulist, 1978) 213.

ing witness par excellence whose testimony is true (21:24). While a real person, the Beloved Disciple functions in the gospel as the embodiment of Johannine idealism: All Christians are disciples and among them greatness is determined by a loving relationship to Jesus, not by function or office.

Finally, even when office is recognized in the Johannine tradition as a pastoral necessity, it is seen through the prism of Johannine values. Chapter 21 (which was probably an epilogue added to the gospel) faces up to the question of ongoing care for those who have been brought into the Christian community by missionary activity (p. 32 above). Earlier John 10:1–18 made it clear that Jesus alone is the model shepherd, while all others are thieves and bandits. What is characteristic and distinctive of his shepherding is not the authority or power he claims over the sheep, but his intimate knowledge of them and love for them. He knows each by name, and they respond when he calls; he is even willing to lay down his life for them. In chap. 21 Peter is assigned the role of tending the sheep[138]—a role of authority which in the last one-third of the first century was being exercised by presbyters in other NT churches and which was being traced back to apostles like Peter and Paul (I Peter 5:1–2: Acts 20:28; *I Clem.* 42:4; 44:1–3). But before Simon Peter is given that role in John 21:15–17, he is first asked insistently (three times!), "Do you love me?" If authority is given, it must be based on love of Jesus. Moreover, Jesus continues to speak of "my lambs, my sheep." The sheep do not belong to Peter or to any human church officer; they continue to belong to the one who said, "I am the model shepherd; I know my sheep and mine know me" (10:14). And if Peter is given a shepherd's task, he must meet Johannine qualifications for shepherding, namely, that "the model shepherd lays down his life for the sheep" (10:11). Therefore, having thrice told Simon Peter to feed/ tend the sheep, in the next breath (21:18–19) Jesus tells him about the way in which he will be put to death. This death will be the proof that, in Peter's role as shepherd, loving discipleship has been given

---

138. The difference between John 10 and John 21 is best explained if one accepts the common theory that 21 was written by another hand. In *Community* I place chap. 21 chronologically after the Epistles and regard it as representative of how a section of the Johannine community moved towards the "Great Church" which already had articulated structure and honored the apostles.

priority: "By this will all identify you as my disciples: by the love that you have for one another. . . . And no one can find greater love than this: that people lay down their lives for those whom they love" (13:35; 15:13).

I have been focusing on how a close reading of the Fourth Gospel shows that discipleship is important, not offices or charisms or other distinctions. Let me call attention to one final instance of Johannine egalitarianism that stands in sharp contrast to the tendencies of the Pastorals. On p. 45 above, I discussed the possibility that in the ecclesiology of those letters the distinction between the teachers and the taught might become fixed rather than flexible, so that the abilities of the larger number of Christians, who constitute "the taught," are not tapped. Those who are not official teachers would often not be trusted to discern truth for themselves. In particular, II Tim 3:1–9 singles out women among the taught as excessively gullible: "They will listen to anybody and can never arrive at the truth." Even if the "they" are not *all*, the categorizing is demeaning; and the practical result is clearly articulated by the "Paul" of I Tim 2:12: "I do not permit a woman to teach or to have authority over a man; rather she must be silent." There was, then, a tendency toward discrimination against women in some NT churches, especially in those churches where community functions were more carefully structured.

Johannine attitudes toward women as seen in the pages of the Fourth Gospel[139] are remarkably different—a difference all the more interesting if the Johannine writings are contemporary with the Pastorals. In chaps. 4, 9, and 11, in full-scale narratives quite unlike any stories in the Synoptic Gospels, John presents scenarios that allow differentiation and development of characters through reaction to Jesus. Therein the Samaritan woman, Martha, and Mary are characters absolutely equal in importance to the blind man and Lazarus. In the portrayal of major male and female believers there is no difference of intelligence, vividness, or response. Martha serves as the spokeswoman of a confession of faith (11:27: "You are the Christ, the Son of God") that is placed on Peter's lips in Matt 16:16–17,

---

139. See my treatment of the "Roles of Women in the Fourth Gospel" in *Community* 183–98.

winning for him from Jesus a blessing and an acknowledgment that divine revelation has been at work. If at the Last Supper the Johannine Jesus prays for those who will believe in him through the word of his (male) disciples (17:20), a whole village comes to believe in Jesus through the word of the Samaritan woman (4:39). In John 20:14 not Peter but Mary Magdalene is the first to see the risen Jesus; and when she goes to the disciples, she is the first to give the Easter proclamation, "I have seen the Lord"—a privilege that won for her in the Middle Ages the designation *apostola apostolorum* (the [woman] apostle unto the apostles). If rank in discipleship is set by Jesus' love, as exemplified in "the Disciple whom Jesus loved," it is said, "Jesus loved Martha and her sister and Lazarus"(11:5). How could the circles from which this Gospel came ever agree in practice with the Pastorals in not allowing women to teach and in suggesting that they never arrive at the truth!

STRENGTHS AND WEAKNESSES

I have traced remarkable consistency in Johannine ecclesiology, stemming from its firm roots in a unique christology. Jesus as God's only Son from before creation is the only source of divine life for human beings. The images of the vine and the shepherd illustrate that it is all important for each person not only to believe in Jesus but to remain attached to him, for he continues as an active life-giver and life-nourisher in the community. Instead of writing of the rule or kingdom of God, John centers all imagery on Jesus as one in whom the reign of God has been perfectly realized, so that inhering in him replaces entrance into the kingdom. Sacraments are signs through which Jesus gives and nourishes life. Church offices and even apostleship are of lesser importance when compared to discipleship which is literally a question of (eternal) life and death. Within that discipleship, there are no second-class Christians; and the love of Jesus alone gives higher status. (In the next chapter I shall show that the picture of the Paraclete-Spirit coheres with this ecclesiology.) What are the strengths and weaknesses of such a powerfully consistent picture?

The **first and greatest strength** comes from the fact that an individual relationship to Jesus on the part of church members is a necessary component of a sound ecclesiology. The ecclesiologies discussed in the preceding chapters all suppose the collectivity of the church. Members of a church should have the sense that they are receiving careful pastoral supervision and trustworthy Christian doctrine (the Pastorals). In moments of crisis, members of a church should have a sense of continuity with a past history in which crises have been survived through the intervention of the Spirit, and with a future history which (even if unknown) lies within God's plan for the evangelization of the world (Acts). Members should have a sense of their dignity that accrues from belonging to the church and of their identity as the people of God (I Peter). Members should have a sense that the church is more than its human components because it is the body of Christ sharing in his holiness (Colossians/Ephesians). But none of these takes the place of a relationship to Jesus. It is true that the body ecclesiology of Colossians/Ephesians gives a clear centrality to Christ, but ironically the Christ who is the head of the body remains faceless. This is because the ecclesiology of Colossians/ Ephesians is in the Pauline heritage; and in his letters Paul (who did not know Jesus in the flesh) does not fill in Jesus' personality. If one had only the Pauline letters, one would be familiar with a few sayings of Jesus and would know that on the night before Jesus died he shared a eucharistic meal with his disciples, that Jesus was crucified and buried, and that Jesus rose on the third day and appeared to designated people. But the kind of person Jesus was and why people followed him during his lifetime never emerges in those letters.[140] Accordingly, although we are told in Colossians/Ephesians that the members of the body receive life from Christ as head and are knit together in love with him, the imagery remains abstract and impersonal. Often it does not satisfy the religious longing to encounter God in a personal way. John's portrayal of Jesus meets that need in an extraordinarily effective way.

---

140. I presume that Paul told his converts much more of the Jesus tradition than is apparent in the problem-oriented letters (and some would detect Jesus information in oblique references in the letters). But we do not know how much of the personal preaching of Paul was known by the authors of Colossians and Ephesians; the latter author shows himself very dependent on the letters. In any case, no more than in the undisputed Pauline letters does the personality of Jesus emerge in Colossians/Ephesians.

In part, this is because John has used the gospel form as the vehicle of his thought and so must bring the mystery of Jesus' ministry into his ecclesiology. I speak of "the mystery" of Jesus' ministry in order to do justice to an element about Jesus' life that escapes discursive description (or, at least, escapes my discursive abilities). Even very skeptical NT critics will admit that in his life Jesus must have impressed people as extraordinary. But the tone of the following of Jesus in the ministry involves more than that—even more than religious awe and veneration. Jesus was remembered as one who exhibited love in what he did and was loved deeply by those who followed him. Detecting love between Jesus and his disciples is not an aberration of nineteenth-century eisegesis; nor is it belied by a tradition of harsh statements by Jesus which may well be authentic. Love was not the whole picture, but it was part of the picture. If we have a right to ask the question that has run through this book, namely, how did the churches survive after the apostles died, we should recognize that there is a prior ecclesiological question: How did the following of Jesus which involved love for him survive after he died? The answer, I suggest, is that it survived only because love for Jesus was looked on as an ongoing element, even among those who never knew him during his ministry. One can argue what Paul meant precisely when he said, "The love of Christ compels us" (II Cor 5:14); yet it is clear that Paul not only believed in Christ but also loved him. (The face of Jesus may not come through in the Pauline letters, but Jesus had a face for Paul.) And so one can make a case that a loving relationship to Jesus, which was a part of the following of Jesus in his lifetime, remains an intrinsic necessity in the church.

That may sound romantic and idealistic but it is surprisingly verifiable in practice. In addition to providing doctrine and pastoral care, liturgy and sacraments, and a supportive sense of belonging to a caring community, a church must bring people into some personal contact with Jesus so that they can experience in their own way what made people follow him in the first place. (Sometimes the term "spirituality" covers this necessary aspect of ecclesiology.) Churches that do this will survive. That Christ willed or founded the church may be adequate theology for some; but an abstraction, focused on the past, will not be enough to keep others loyal to a church unless they encounter Jesus there. They will join small groups where they find an encounter with Jesus, even if these are tangential to or separated from the church. At the beginning of this chapter I made an oblique reference to an exaggerated form of Christian individualism—a "Jesus and me" pattern that makes the people of God almost irrelevant. The very attraction that such exaggerated individualism has for people points up the need for having a personal, loving relationship to Jesus as a component in a larger Christian picture.

In Roman Catholic parishes that have taken the changes of Vatican II seriously there is often much more participation of parishioners in liturgy and in parish life in general. It is all the more startling, then, for pastors of such active parishes to find they are losing parishioners to religious groups that stress a personal relationship to Jesus, basing themselves on the Scriptures (sometimes fundamentalistically interpreted). Such pastors will argue correctly that there cannot be a church unless there is a worshiping community; but they are finding that worship in itself, without an accompanying personal spirituality, does not hold some people. The church, even in liturgical celebration, can seem abstracted from the Jesus described in the gospel pages. (See the dichotomy I mentioned on p. 88 above.) If this happens in the green wood, what about the dry? How much more will the large impersonal parishes of any denomination lose parishioners, not only because the parishioners have no active sense of belonging to community from which to derive a sense of identity (p. 79 above), but also because they do not encounter Jesus in the church. "Born-again Christians" is sometimes used pejoratively by mainline church members to describe people so impressed by an individual salvific relationship to Jesus that it seems to constitute their whole ecclesiology. There is no doubt that John is the gospel par excellence of such "Born-again" enthusiasts. Nevertheless, I would argue that John has a corrective role to play in the mainline churches when it is read critically rather than harmonistically. It can remind them, as it did Christians in the first century, that church membership is not a sufficient goal, for the church must lead to Jesus. Church members receive life from being attached to Jesus and must be in a loving relationship to him.

The main weakness of this thrust in Johannine ecclesiology is already inherent in what I said above. Taken by itself, without the Jewish context of collectivity inherited from Israel, John tends to foster Christian individualism to the point where a sense of the church is lost. (It is no accident that the term "the church" in the wide sense does not occur in the Johannine writings.[141]) When John is read to support the "Jesus is my personal savior" mentality, a logical derivative of that for some may be that they really need no community, no share in a people, no liturgy, no sacraments. Pietistic groups for which certain passages in John make it *the* gospel should reflect on the Pastorals, Colossians/Ephesians, and I Peter as a corrective.

A **second strength** in Johannine ecclesiology is its egalitarianism, i.e., the sense of equality among the members of the community. We saw that disciple is the most important category, and there is no evidence that either charisms or offices give status. In other NT churches, whether they rejoice in charisms (apostles, prophets, teachers, etc., in I Cor 12:28) or have developed regular offices (the presbyter-bishops and deacons of the Pastorals), there is a tendency to give one charism or one office precedence over another. That development is, in part, consciously or unconsciously, by imitation of secular societies; and inevitably, as in secular societies, precedence will be equated with value. We find an echo of this in various gospel passages correcting the attempts of members of the Twelve to have the first place in the kingdom or to be the greatest (Mark 9:33–37; 10:35–40; and par.). That attempt is not recorded in the Fourth Gospel; ambition is not a factor if all are disciples and precedence or status comes from the love of Jesus. In fact the author of III John 9 shows an abhorrence for Diotrephes who seems to be trying to introduce something like episcopal office into Johannine ecclesiology.[142] Says the Johannine writer with contempt, "He likes to be first among them"; and throughout the ages many Christians have shared this dislike for the inevitable ambition produced by a structured church. On the other side of the coin, the Johannine corrective is perhaps more important today when many feel they are second-class citizens in the church because they do *not* have authority—a tacit acknowledgment of how important in the church power has become. Both

---

141. In the Johannine gospel and epistles the word *ekklēsia* occurs only in III John 6,9,10 where it clearly refers to local churches.

142. For the complicated issue of what Diotrephes was doing, see my *Epistles* 107, 732–38.

those who are ambitious for authority and those who are sad because
they do not possess it have not understood the lesson of the vine and
the branches.

There is a special problem in the churches that have an ordained
priesthood in their church structure. In discussing I Peter above (p.
81), I pointed out that the presence of an ordained priesthood can
have the unfortunate side-effect of minimalizing an appreciation of
the priesthood of all believers.[143] In relation to the equality of Christians as disciples, it is especially difficult for the ordained priesthood
to be kept in the category of service (to God and to the community),
for the ordained will frequently be assumed to be more important
and automatically more holy. Because ordination is seen as a sacrament and priests deal with sacred things, they are frequently regarded as better than ordinary Christians. In my own church some would
find surprising this almost elementary affirmation: the day when a
person is baptized is more important than the day when a person is
ordained priest and bishop. The first sacrament, after all, touches on
salvation; it constitutes one a child of God, a dignity that goes beyond designation to the special service of God. Recent Popes have
laudably resigned one trapping of royalty after the other related to
installation in papal office, e.g., the tiara crown, coronation, etc. I
wonder what impression a future Pope might make upon being elect-
ed if he decided not to accept a special regnal name but to retain his
baptismal name, explaining that he wanted to be known to the
church by the name by which he was sealed as a Christian and made
known to Jesus Christ. That gesture might remove a wrong sense of
papal claims shared by many outsiders, for it would demonstrate the
belief that *salvifically* an identity as a Christian is more important
than an identity gained from authority. Such a suggestion detracts
not at all from the legitimate authority of the vicar of Peter recognized in my church; rather it contemporizes what John was trying to
say by comparing the Beloved Disciple with Peter.

---

143. My pointing out difficulties about an ordained *priesthood* here and on p. 81
above (as distinct from ordained *ministry*) does not mean I think that the Roman
Catholic Church can or should dispense with the priestly understanding of the ministry. In *Critical Meaning* 102–6 I point out the enormous strength and value of this
priesthood. Ordination is not just appointment to a job; it entails special grace. But see
p. 37 above for limitations to every theological strength.

There are other facets of strength and weakness in Johannine ecclesiology, but it would be better if they were left until we discuss the role of the Paraclete-Spirit and follow out the story of Johannine Christianity into the Epistles.

CHAPTER 7

The Heritage of the Beloved Disciple and the Epistles of John: A Community of Individuals Guided by the Paraclete-Spirit

A VERY IMPORTANT ASPECT of Johannine ecclesiology remains to be treated, namely the role of the Spirit under the title of Paraclete. In order, however, to understand the import of the Paraclete in Johannine self-understanding and the subsequent fate of the Johannine community as illustrated by the Epistles of John, one needs at least a brief sketch of the history underlying the Fourth Gospel.

The disciples who follow Jesus in John 1:35–51 include names known in the other gospels (Andrew, Peter, Philip); and the titles given to Jesus there are found in the other gospels (Messiah, Son of God, King, Son of Man). It would seem, then, that at least in its origins Johannine Christianity was not too distant from the dominant style of Christianity in the movement centered on Jesus. In chap. 4 of John, however, Samaritans are being converted (but not by the original disciples of Jesus); and Temple worship in Jerusalem is declared as losing its significance. Here John has departed significantly from the description of the ministry in the other gospels and is closer to the developments described in Acts 6–8. There (without a break of communion) Hellenist Jewish Christians[144] separate administratively from the Hebrew Christian majority in Jerusalem who are faithful to the Temple observances; and (in the person of Stephen) Hellenist preaching proclaims that God does not dwell in the Temple. These Hellenist Christians, not Peter or the Twelve, are the ones who convert Samaria. I contend that Johannine Christianity consisted not only of the type of Hebrew Christians whose heritage is preserved in many other NT works, but also of groups similar to the Hellenists, more radical in their attitudes toward Judaism. There were also Samaritan converts.[145] As I explained in detail in *Community,* this mixture may have hastened innovative developments in Johannine christology and made Johannine Christians particularly troublesome in the eyes of Jews who did not believe in Jesus. (The typical Johannine terminology for the opponents of Jesus, namely, "the Jews," which would be inappropriate on the lips of Jesus during his lifetime, is explicable as the influence of a Samaritan component in the Johannine tradition.)

In any case, beginning in chap. 5 a dominant theme of the Johannine account of Jesus' ministry is the hatred that "the Jews" have for Jesus because he is making himself God. The divinity of Jesus as one who had come down from God[146] (an aspect of divinity not apparent in the other gospels—see p. 85 above) is publicly spoken of

---

144. From the implications of Acts one can reconstruct the features that distinguished Hellenist Christians from Hebrew Christians, but only with some uncertainty. There are the added problems of the accuracy of Acts and of whether this distinction described in Jerusalem existed elsewhere and in the same way. See Brown and Meier, *Antioch* 6–7, 34.

145. In John 8:48 Jesus is mocked as a Samaritan. Nothing verifiable in his life would warrant that, and so it may echo a charge against Johannine Christianity. The presence of many Samaritans among those who believed in Jesus is a tradition peculiar to John (4:39–42) among the gospels.

146. Many factors entered into shaping this expression of christology, especially reflection on pre-existent divine Wisdom as described in late OT and in intertestamental literature (Brown, *John* 1.521–23). Another factor may have been an emphasis on Moses rather than on David as the prime OT analogue for understanding Jesus. Moses was a figure who was famous not because he *became* king (as David did) but because he spoke with God, perhaps even saw God, and then *came down* to tell people what he heard and saw when he was with God. The Samaritans rejected the Davidic claims centered around Jerusalem and held on to the covenant with Moses who was for them the principal figure in sacred history.

and attacked. There are long debates between Jesus and "the Jews" that grow increasingly hostile. What lies beneath the surface becomes apparent in the story of the man born blind in John 9. The Jews in anger say, "We are the disciples of Moses; we know that God has spoken to Moses. As for that fellow [Jesus], we do not even know where he comes from" (9:28–29). The man born blind, who is described by them as one of the disciples of "that fellow," also speaks as a "we": "We know that God pays no attention to sinners . . . if this man [Jesus] were not from God, he could have done nothing" (9:31,33). The synagogue and the Johannine community are thus alienated from each other as disciples of Moses and disciples of Jesus; and through the medium of struggles in Jesus' own life, the struggles between these two groups are being told. (In other words the Fourth Gospel narrates on two levels: the level of Jesus' life and the level of the community's life.[147]) Just as the man born blind is put on trial before the Pharisees or "the Jews," so have members of the Johannine community been put on trial by synagogue leaders. Just as the man born blind is ejected from the synagogue for confessing that Jesus has come from God, so have the Johannine Christians been ejected from the synagogue for their confession of Jesus (see also 16:2). And in the course of this synagogue action which was looked upon as a persecution, Johannine Christians have been put to death, either directly by the Jewish authorities or indirectly by being denounced to Roman authorities (15:20; 16:2–3). To this treatment the oratorical reaction by the Johannine Jesus is bitter: those Jews who are trying to kill him are the children of the devil who was a murderer from the beginning (8:40,44).

To have suffered expulsion from the synagogue because of a belief that Jesus had come from God inevitably sharpened and tightened the adherence of Johannine Christians to their high christology. Jesus is so much one with Father (10:30) that he is not only Lord but also God (20:28). Over such issues the Johannine Christians were willing to criticize sharply even other Christians. There is contempt in the Fourth Gospel for Jews who *believed* in Jesus but who were unwilling to confess it openly lest they be put out of the synagogue

---

147. Very good on this is J. L. Martyn, *History & Theology in the Fourth Gospel* (2nd ed.; Nashville: Abingdon, 1979).

(12:42). There is hostility towards Jewish disciples who have followed Jesus openly but who object when it is said that he has come down from heaven and can give his flesh to eat (6:60–66)[148] or because he is described as existing before Abraham (8:58). Such criticism of others suggests that the Johannine Christians must have been extremely controversial because of their christology, challenged both by Jews who did not believe in Jesus and by Jews who did believe in him. The courtroom atmosphere of the Fourth Gospel with its constant stress on testimony/witness, accusation, and judgment (1:19–21; 5:31–47; 7:50–51; 8:14–18; etc.) and with its debates over the implications of Scripture texts (6:31–33; 7:40–43,52; 10:34–36) reflects the controversies and how they were conducted.

The struggle with the synagogue and the resultant polemic atmosphere are very important in understanding what is present in John but also what is absent. The synagogue leaders apparently thought that the Johannine confession of Jesus as God denied the basic faith of Israel: "The Lord our God is one." In response the evangelist defended the divinity of Jesus so massively that the Fourth Gospel scarcely allows for human limitation.[149] Jesus cannot ask a simple question without a Johannine footnote explaining that he already knew the answer (6:5–6). Jesus cannot choose a follower who goes bad without Johannine insistence that he foresaw this from the beginning (6:70–71). Jesus cannot utter a prayer of petition without the assurance that he is only educating the bystanders to the truth that the Father always hears him (11:41–42). Jesus cannot ask that the hour of the passion pass from him (as he does in the other gospels), for his coming to the hour is intentional (12:27). The passion of Jesus cannot be narrated in a way that would place him at the mercy of his captors, for he has sovereign power to lay down his life and take it up again (10:18; see 18:6). The entire presentation protects Jesus from whatever could be a challenge to divinity. If asked whether

---

148. In John's outlook, Jesus' brothers may have been among these; for although they supported him on the surface, they did not believe in him (7:3–5). By the end of the century, James, "the brother of the Lord" (see Gal 1:19), had become the hero of Jewish Christians who remained observant of most Jewish customs.

149. "The Word became flesh and made his dwelling among us" (1:14) does *not* stress limitations, for the verse continues, "We have seen his glory, the glory of an only Son coming from the Father."

Jesus was human, the Johannine evangelist might well have answered, "Of course; he walked among us." But the evangelist does
not stress that humanity since it was never queried by the synagogue
polemicists. Similarly, ethical or moral directives are almost totally
absent from John—there is nothing like the Sermon on the Mount of
Matthew—almost surely because such basics as the commandments
were not a matter of dispute between the Johannine community and
the synagogue. A fuller portrait of Jesus may have been presupposed
by the evangelist; but what he painted is somewhat monochromatic,
since the struggle with the synagogue limited the palette to black and
white.

The uniqueness of the Johannine concept of the Paraclete-Spirit,
which I shall now develop, is also fully intelligible only in the context
of Johannine polemical history given above. Although early Christians could agree on the importance of the Spirit, they had very different notions of what was meant by that term (see ftnote 94 above).
Because the Greek *pneuma* is neuter and the Spirit is referred to as
"it" in NT writings, we have difficulty in determining to what extent
Paul or Acts or I Peter considered the Spirit as personal. But once
again christology has had a powerful impact on John's views, for in
the Last Supper account of the Fourth Gospel[150] the Spirit is to come
from God after Jesus has returned to the Father. The replacement
motif is so strong that almost everything said about the Spirit has already been said about Jesus. The Spirit emerges clearly as a personal
presence—the ongoing presence of Jesus while he is absent from
earth and with the Father in heaven.

For this concept of the Spirit there appears (in the Fourth Gospel alone [151]) a designation that is not neuter, *paraklētos*, enabling the
Spirit to be the antecedent of personal pronouns. In its root meaning
the Greek term means "called [*klētos*] alongside [*para*]"; and like its
Latin equivalent *advocatus* ("called [*vocatus*] to [*ad*]"), it has a foren-

---

150. All the references to the Spirit as Paraclete occur in five passages in John's
Last Supper account: 14:15–17; 14:25–26; 15:26–27; 16:7–11; 16:12–15. For a detailed
discussion and for bibliography pertinent to what I sketch above, see Brown, *John*
2.1135–44.

151. *Paraklētos* occurs in I John 2:1: "We have a Paraclete in the presence of the
Father, Jesus Christ the Just One." Jesus is the first Paraclete and he serves as an
advocate in heaven; the Spirit is "another Paraclete" (John 14:16) and he serves on
earth after Jesus has gone.

sic or legal use. When people are in trouble, they call in a lawyer or counsellor or *advocate* to stand beside them in court. The legal context fits the Johannine history I have described wherein the members of the community had to defend themselves for their christological views. Their help and surety was the Paraclete-Spirit dwelling within them who interpreted correctly the significance of Jesus. Indeed, through them and their witness the Paraclete went over to the attack and proved the world wrong, showing that true justice was on Jesus' side (16:8–11). Another reason for which the Spirit is "called alongside" is consolation at times of trouble, whence the Consoler or Holy Comforter. In the context of the Last Supper Jesus is going away. Although this makes the hearts of his disciples sorrowful, it is better that he goes away; for then the Paraclete comes (16:6–7), and they have the consolation of one who more than makes up for Jesus' departure. Jesus lived on this earth in one time in one area; the Paraclete dwells within every believer for all times (14:15–17). Thus the Paraclete is a more intimate and enduring presence. It should now be clear why in discussing Johannine ecclesiology, we may see the Paraclete concept as another facet of John's emphasis on the relationship of the individual to Jesus. Just as Jesus represents on earth the Father who sent him, the Paraclete represents on earth Jesus who sent him. Jesus said, "Whoever has seen me has seen the Father" (14:9); it would be equally possible for the Johannine Jesus to say, "Whoever has received the Paraclete has received me" (see 14:17).

An especially emphasized aspect of the representative role of the Paraclete is as a teacher. In 14:15–17 Jesus says to his disciples, "If you love me and keep my commandments, then at my request the Father will give you another Paraclete . . . the Spirit of Truth."[152] He continues, "The Paraclete, the Holy Spirit that the Father will send in my name will teach you everything and remind you of all that I told you" (14:26). "When the Spirit of Truth comes, he will guide

---

152. "The Spirit of Truth" (14:17; 15:26; 16:13; I John 4:6) is, like "Paraclete," a designation peculiar to the Johannine writings in the NT. In the Qumran Dead Sea Scrolls it describes the leader of the good forces—an angelic spirit, but also a spirit in which the good walk. One may say the truth-and-light figure envisaged in Essene Judaism as the chief opponent of Belial (the Spirit of Falsehood, the leader of darkness) has bifurcated in Christianity, with Jesus as the light and truth visibly manifested, and the Holy Spirit as indwelling truth.

you along the way of all truth. For he will not speak on his own, but will speak only what he hears and will declare to you the things to come. He will glorify me because it is from me that he will receive what he will declare to you" (16:13–14). Jesus has received everything he had to say from the Father, but he contemporized this revelation by proclaiming it to his disciples on earth. The Paraclete will receive everything he has to say from Jesus; but, dwelling in the heart of each Christian, he will contemporize it in each period and in each place, thus enabling Christians to face the things to come. The Johannine approach meets an acute problem. If Christianity is to be apostolic, it must pass on what was received from Jesus by the first generation; it must guard a tradition. If Christianity is to face new situations meaningfully, it must have an element of the contemporary and the original. The Paraclete preserves the past without corruption because he receives everything from Jesus and gives no new revelation. Yet he is a living teacher who does not just repeat a tradition of the dead past. If the presbyter-bishops of the Pastorals were supposed to teach by holding firm to what had been taught to them (Titus 1:9), the Paraclete not only declares what he has received from Jesus (John 16:14) but through that medium also declares the things to come (16:13). If one seeks an example of what is meant by the old and the new in the teaching role ascribed to the Paraclete, one may look at the Fourth Gospel itself. That constitutes the witness borne by the Paraclete through the Beloved Disciple and through the evangelist. It is a gospel, like the other gospels, centered on the public activity of Jesus leading up to his death and resurrection; but it presents that story in a truly innovative way so that every page is transformed by the unique Johannine perception of christology (p. 85 above).

STRENGTHS AND WEAKNESSES

The Paraclete-Spirit concept contributes **strength** to Johannine ecclesiology. Because Jesus came from or was sent by the Father and spoke only what he heard when he was with Him, he was sovereign in all the hostile debates with "the Jews." Because the Paraclete came from the Father (15:26), was sent by Jesus (16:7), and speaks only what he heard from Jesus (16:13), the Johannine community that bears witness through him (15:27) is unchallengeable in its christology. Those Jews or other Christians who debate skeptically with the christology of pre-existence proclaimed by the Johannine witness-bearers are really disbelieving the "I am" of Jesus himself. The death of the great figures of the first generation who had seen the earthly or risen Jesus, whether apostles or not, cannot weaken the confidence of Johannine Christians in the correctness of their ongoing perceptions. (Indeed, not even the death of the Beloved Disciple can do that.) The figures of that first generation bore significant witness, but only because they possessed the Paraclete; and this same Paraclete remains on in the hearts of the second and third generation of Johannine Christians.

In the preceding chapter I stressed Johannine egalitarianism: there are no second-class Christians *in terms of status*; all are disciples, and that is what really matters. The idea that God would be worshiped neither in Jerusalem nor on the Samaritan mountain but in Spirit and truth (4:21–23) means that there are no second-class Christians *geographically.* God is Spirit (4:24), and the Spirit of Truth dwells in every Christian everywhere. The idea that the Paraclete is given to each person who loves Jesus and keeps his commandments and thus remains forever (14:15–16) means that there are no second-class Christians *chronologically.* True, they were privileged who saw Jesus and believed, but blessed are those who have not seen Jesus and have believed (20:29). Jesus prays for those who believed during the ministry (17:8–9), but Jesus also prays for later generations who believe through their word (17:20). Thus, Johannine ecclesiology is without any barriers of status, space, or time that could make some more distant from Jesus than others.

Nevertheless, this attractive picture of Johannine church attitudes is marred by what happened. In this instance, we do not have to guess what bad results might flow from the main stresses in John's ecclesiology, for the Johannine Epistles show the tragic aftereffects. Let me first analyze the situation reflected in these epistles,[153] and

---

153. The substantiation for all that follows may be found in my *Epistles;* see in particular the brief statement of my theory about these works given there on pp. 69–71.

then relate it to the history of the Johannine community I have described earlier in this chapter.

Situation in the Epistles. Written no more than a decade after the Fourth Gospel, the Johannine Epistles reflect a startling change in the community situation. No longer is there concern with the Jews or with other groups of Christian believers who are not adequate in their faith. The whole focus is on a secession from within the community, so serious that it is described in apocalyptic language: "You heard that Antichrist is to come: well, now many Antichrists have made their appearance, and this makes us certain that it really is the last hour. It was from our ranks that they went out—not that they really belonged to us; for if they had belonged to us, they would have remained with us" (I John 2:18–19). The epistolary author[154] is writing so urgently not because he hopes these false prophets (4:1) will read his work and be convinced, but because they are conducting an ongoing missionary effort undermining the adherence of his followers. He is hoping through his writing to stem their success, for the whole world is listening to them (4:5). The issue comes to a head in II John which is a warning addressed to an outlying community not yet affected by the secession. "The deceivers who have gone out into the world" (II John 7) are going to come to that community, and so the author beseeches the Christians there not even to allow such people through the door of the house church (II John 10).

It is not easy to decipher the thought of the secessionists, for we must reconstruct it from the criticisms leveled by the epistolary author and from his own professions of faith.[155] He assumes that his readers know the issues in dispute and is more concerned with refutation than with clear exposition. My commentary on *The Epistles of John* surveys the different scholarly views about the thought of the secessionists; here, in brief, is what I think makes most sense.

The secessionists are progressive innovators (II John 9) in the eyes of an author who considers himself conservative, holding on to what was taught from the beginning (I John 3:11a). He associates

---

154. I posit one author for all three epistles who is distinct from the evangelist of the Fourth Gospel.

155. In an appendix to my *Epistles,* 762–63, I have listed all the epistolary statements that would enable us to reconstruct the seccessionist thought.

himself with a chain of Johannine witnesses reaching back to the Beloved Disciple—a "we" who have seen and heard Jesus (I John 1:1–4). *Christologically*, the secessionists are accused of neglecting the "flesh" or humanity of Jesus (I John 4:2; II John 7). Presumably this means that they did not place salvific importance on what was, after all, only a phase of the pre-existent Word. As former community members, the secessionists, in fidelity to John 1:14, would have admitted an incarnation. But the very entrance of Jesus, the light, into the world was what gave eternal life to those who believe (John 3:16–17); his subsequent deeds, including his death, would not have been important. *Ethically*, the secessionists would see the only sin to consist in refusing to believe in Jesus. The believer is a child of God, is already judged (John 3:18; 5:24) and already has eternal life. Therefore, while not encouraging libertinism, the secessionists would have proclaimed that there is no salvific value in doing good deeds or obeying commandments, and there is no sin provided one believes (I John 1:8,10). Against such christological and ethical views, the author would claim that from the beginning it had been known that salvation came not only from the incarnation of the Word but also from Jesus' death as an essential component. Jesus came "not in water only but in water and blood" (I John 5:6). The supreme love of God was that he sent His Son into the world, true, but as an atonement for our sins (4:9–10); and that atonement was accomplished through the blood of Jesus which cleanses us from sins (1:7). The way Jesus "walked" on earth was very important, not only christologically but also ethically, since we must walk as he walked (1:7), make ourselves pure as he was pure (3:3), avoid sin as he was sinless (3:5–6), act justly as he was just (3:7). Commandments are very important, for "the person who keeps God's commandments abides in God" (3:24). By no means does the epistolary author deny that through faith and baptism we receive God's eternal life, but there is still a future development. "Yes, beloved, we are God's children right now; but what we shall be has not yet been revealed" (3:2). That revelation comes through a final judgment before which we must be careful not to be ashamed by what we have done (2:28 – 3:2).

How the epistolary situation developed from the Fourth Gospel. Such a bitter schism reflecting antithetical views of Christianity is clearly a church tragedy. What we are interested in is how the

schism developed from the Fourth Gospel, as illustrative of the
weaknesses inherent in the attractive christology and ecclesiology of
that magnificent writing. The thesis I have attempted to defend with
rigor in my commentary on *The Epistles of John* is that both the author and the secessionists accepted the presentation of Jesus in the
Fourth Gospel (whether they knew that presentation in written or
oral form). Few scholars have doubted that the epistolary author
drew on previous Johannine tradition; but I would argue that, even
though the secessionists are described as "progressives," every idea
they had (as reconstructed from the polemic of I and II John) can be
plausibly explained as derivative from the Johannine tradition. The
whole dispute, then, is over the interpretation of a commonly accepted tradition.

That fact casts light for me on **four weaknesses** inherent in the
tradition because it was shaped by polemic and because it claimed
unchallengeable guidance by the Paraclete. Noting these weaknesses
is particularly important for ecumenical discussions today between
Protestants and Roman Catholics, for the sixteenth-century division
was also bitterly polemic, involved excommunication and accusa-
tions of being Antichrists, and sought to justify positions through appeal to the Spirit and to the common scriptures. If we learn some of
the problems of the first-century division, we may learn some of the
problems of that of the sixteenth—and of the twentieth.

FIRST WEAKNESS: the one-sidedness of a theology shaped in polemic, ultimately leading to exaggeration and division. I pointed out
above that the evangelist emphasized in the Fourth Gospel what
"the Jews" and other Christians denied: the pre-existent divinity of
Jesus. Being put on trial and suffering for this faith lent a brilliant
clarity to the presentation. Readers ever since have come away convinced, as the author intended, that they must believe that Jesus is
the Christ, the Son of God, and that believing they gain life in his
name (John 20:31). That was splendid so long as this Gospel was read
by Johannine Christians who took it for granted that Jesus was human; that while the incarnation brought light into the world, the
light could not be fully perceived until after the death and resurrection; and that belief in Jesus necessarily entailed an ongoing commitment to live in a manner worthy of that belief. The emphasis that
belief or refusal of belief constitutes the judgment made sense, so

long as it was proclaimed in a context where Jesus' ultimate return as judge was simply taken for granted—a return that would show up self-deception in the status of those who claimed to be believers. But when a theology such as that of the Fourth Gospel has been shaped in polemic and the people who held on to it have been traumatically expelled by the opponents (in this case by the Jews of the synagogue), the trauma tends to obscure the presuppositions; and *often what is passed on to the next generation is only what was fought over.* If a major document was written at the general time of the trauma to state the case for those who suffered (as the Fourth Gospel did brilliantly), that document will tend to become *the* foundational document of the next generation, *the* Bible to be rehearsed. Therefore, for the next Johannine generation the one-sidedness of the Fourth Gospel could and did become a stumbling stone for those who did not know the presuppositions.[156]

The reason why the epistolary author must reach back to "the beginning" to refute the secessionists is because there is perilously little in the Fourth Gospel itself to refute them. They read about a Jesus who *during his public ministry* offered eternal life to those who believed that he was the light come into the world, sent by the Father. How would readers without a traditional background know that such eternal life became a possibility only after Jesus died for our sins (as the epistolary author claims)? Yes, there is a statement about "the Lamb of God who takes away the world's sin" (John 1:29). Unless the secessionists knew earlier tradition, however, would they catch subtle references in the Fourth Gospel to Jesus *dying* as a passover lamb,[157] and would they not assume that the very coming into the world took away the world's sin, since the statement appears

---

156. It is possible that not only the passing of time but also a geographical move distanced the next generation from the presuppositions of the preceding generation. Although the Johannine community probably began in Palestine, the Fourth Gospel was written elsewhere (probably in the Ephesus region in my judgment, but some opt for Syria).

157. Jesus was sentenced to death at noon on the eve of Passover (John 19:14), the time when the slaughter of the Passover lambs began in the Temple. When Jesus cried, "I thirst," they put a sponge full of sour wine on hyssop and held it to his mouth (19:28–29)—in Egypt hyssop was used to smear the Israelite doorposts with the blood of the lamb. None of Jesus' bones were broken, according to the prescription for the Passover lamb (19:33,36).

at the beginning of the public ministry? The Johannine Christians who were expelled from the synagogue took with them the moral sense of Judaism that God must be served by living out His covenant commandments. Yet would the Jewish horror of sin as a breaking of covenant commandments have been felt by the next generation if they memorized the Fourth Gospel which talks only about the sin of not believing?

I need not belabor the point. The Fourth Gospel produced by polemic is like a diamond that has been made brilliant by the strokes of the cutter, but only the side thus polished catches the eye. Controversy made this Gospel exciting and attractive but uneven. By contrast, Luke/Acts is a less exciting work theologically but more balanced. I suspect that Luther's theology would have been much less interesting and forcefully attractive if he had not been opposed. The hostile reaction of Rome in excommunicating him helped to bring the issues into lucid clarity for him and for others, so that people had to decide for or against. The language of *krisis*, "judgment, crisis," so endemic in the Fourth Gospel, catches the thrust of the issue. Those who adhere to such a theology as John's have to face a crisis and to make a judgment, and their proclamation of the theology will cause others to make a judgment by taking a stand with or against them.

In the sequence consisting of forming a challenging theological position, encountering polemic, being expelled or excommunicated,[158] and adamantly intensifying the theological position, there will be a further step, namely, dividing internally over the very point that originally led to the polemic and the expulsion. Some within the expelled group will press the crucial point farther than others. It is almost as if the excommunication loosens all brakes on the inner dynamism of the movement. If Johannine community members felt deeply enough about the pre-existent divinity of Jesus to be expelled from the synagogue on the charge of worshiping another God, and if that expulsion made them more adamant, so that in the description of Jesus they avoided human features that might supply the syna-

---

158. Johannine community members were thrown out of the synagogue (John 9:34; 16:2), but we are not certain whether there was any formal excommunication such as described in later Jewish law.

gogue with ammunition against them, inevitably some member would go further in downplaying the humanity altogether, causing horror among others who thought this was going too far. It had taken tremendous courage to split from the synagogue; it would take less courage for a further split to take place within the group itself. I used above the imagery of a diamond being polished by the chisel-and-hammer blows of opposition; the danger is that a final blow splits the diamond itself because of an internal flaw.

For the author of the Johannine Epistles, the secessionists have gone out from the community by moving too progressively. One can be sure that, for the secessionists, the author and his adherents were at fault, not seeing the dynamism of the community insights and attempting to freeze them at a particular stage. The author contended that he was holding on to the tradition as it was understood from the beginning; the secessionists probably claimed they were exemplifying the thrust that produced the tradition in the first place. I think once more of a Luther divided from Rome on the question of merit and claiming that his insights were justified by the Scriptures, despite all Rome's appeal to authority and tradition to the contrary. Inevitably, there came a more radical movement arguing that Luther had retained features that were not in the Scriptures and was not faithful to the thrust of his own insights about the supremacy of the Bible.

SECOND WEAKNESS: the unbridgeable chasm resulting from polemics and expulsion, leading to a loss of heritage. It is tragic that within a group expelled after polemic confrontation, schism often occurs as some push to exaggeration. It is perhaps even more tragic that the expulsion itself tends to open up such a wide gap from the parent group that much of a heritage that was never in dispute is now lost. Despite the differences caused by their insistence on the pre-existent divinity of Jesus, the Johannine community of Christians had more in common religiously with the synagogue Jews who expelled them than with the pagan religious world in which they lived. They shared with the synagogue Jews a belief in one God, the Scriptures, liturgical feasts, the basic ethics of the Law, etc. Yet soon after the expulsion, one reads in the Fourth Gospel, in reference to the Jews, the expression "their Law" (John 15:25) as if the Law of the OT (actually, in this instance, the Psalms) did not belong to Christians as well. The great feasts of Passover and Tabernacles are in

John feasts "of the Jews" and alien to Christians. There is a division between the disciples of Moses and the disciples of Jesus (the "that fellow" of John 9:28), as if the disciples of Jesus were not also disciples of Moses. In other words, the great common heritage is disappearing from view as the points of division sharpen.[159]

The gap will tend to widen if there is an internal split among those expelled, with some pushing to the point of exaggeration the community's theological insight that caused the difficulty in the first place. Such exaggeration confirms the leaders of the parent group that they acted rightly in expelling, and that they diagnosed correctly the implications of the group's theology. (The question is rarely raised whether such exaggeration would have occurred if there had been no expulsion.) One can guess that if the synagogue leaders heard of the inner-Johannine secession, they would have regarded the secessionists as the inevitable result of the wild thoughts about Jesus propounded by the fourth evangelist. The appearance of the *Schwärmerei* or the more radical Protestants surely confirmed Rome in its judgment that Luther's movement was destined to produce anarchy.

A final step occurs when the parent group and those expelled, who once had so much in common, become two different religions. Ironically they may then be embarrassed, defensive, or sensitive about any remaining points in common. For instance, by mid-second century the great remaining heritage that Jews and Christians had in common was the OT (after Marcion's attempt to get rid of that failed); but they could not agree on interpreting the OT and accused each other of distorting or falsifying it! Similarly, a few decades into the Reformation period, Protestants were very sensitive about features that were redolent of their Catholic heritage, so that practices that never bothered Luther or even Zwingli (frequency of eucharist, devotion to Mary) began to be suspect. On the Catholic side, to give emphasis to Bible reading was looked on as Protestant and suspect.

---

159. In this respect the appearance of the Augsburg Confession a decade into the Reformation is remarkable. That confession began by reminding Lutherans and Catholics of the many points they had in common before it came to the relatively few points on which there was serious disagreement. Alas, it failed to heal the breach.

Indeed, reforms that surely would have been introduced into Catholicism had there been no Reformation (liturgy in the vernacular) were postponed indefinitely because they were identified as Protestantizing.

I have insisted in this book that for every theological insight one pays a price. The more brilliant the insight, the more likely that other aspects of truth will be put into the shade, often to be overlooked and forgotten. A balanced religious group, sufficiently confident of its great insights, is not afraid peacefully to look back in order to reclaim what was lost by the very fact that it urged those insights so strongly. But where polemic had been the midwife in bringing to birth a community's identifying insights, the possibility of reaching back to regain some of the lost heritage is significantly diminished. In such a situation self-identity has been fortified by propaganda against the lost values as if they were worthless. In the Fourth Gospel Jesus is presented as speaking on the principal feasts of the Jews, replacing their significance with claims he makes about his own gifts.[160] How, then, can the members of the community shaped by this Gospel ever ask themselves about liturgical values lost when they were expelled from the synagogue? In a more recent example, the polemics were so sharp in the Reformation era that 450 years passed before Protestants and Catholics could enter meaningful dialogue as to how both had truncated their heritage by polemics. And to this day extremists on the two sides regard such dialogue as betraying the cause.

A less dramatic example of the problem of loss of heritage has been brought home to Roman Catholics by Vatican II. There was little *public* polemic in the Council, as changes were made in basic attitudes toward liturgy, law, and lifestyle. But Roman Catholicism suffered from the suddenness and dramatic quality of the changes, so that polemics followed the Council; and a Catholicism marked by the dramatic shift of Vatican II was passed on to the next generation. The new developments that had affected the lives of the teachers

---

160. In chap. 5 he speaks on the occasion of the Sabbath; in chap. 6 on Passover; in chaps. 7 – 9 on Tabernacles; in chap. 10 on Dedication or Hanukkah. See Brown, *John* 1.201-4.

were the substance of the message communicated to the children, but concomitantly this involved a neglect of much Catholic tradition that was *not* affected by the Council—the distinctive presuppositions of Catholic life. As a result the generation that grew up in the 1970s, while being very aware of some new outlooks of Vatican II, were often painfully ignorant of much of their Catholic heritage. Those who taught the new were at times deaf to cries about the loss of the old, equating all such cries with a traditionalist rejection of the Council. There were and are extremist Catholics opposed to Vatican II, either openly (like Archbishop Lefebvre) or covertly (by constantly citing pre-conciliar documents that point in a direction opposite to Vatican II). But others, and I would include myself among them, while enthusiastic for what was introduced into Catholicism by Vatican II, see no need for the concomitant losses, e.g., of inner-Catholic loyalty, obedience, and commitment to the church; of dignity in liturgy; of Gregorian chant; of a knowledge of the Latin tradition reaching from Augustine through Thomas to the Middle Ages. To try now to recoup some of those losses while still advancing the gains of Vatican II would be an act of eminent good sense. Let us hope that the bitterness of the exchanges between extremists does not prevent that. Recouping was what the author of the Johannine Epistles was trying to do in the aftermath of the brilliant Fourth Gospel period in Johannine community history. Never once does he deny the insights of the Fourth Gospel, but he seeks to frame those insights in the context of the presuppositions that the evangelist had probably taken for granted but never mentioned or stressed. By his efforts the epistolary author proved to later church theologians that the Fourth Gospel (which during the second century was the focal point of gnostic commentators) was capable of serving orthodox Christianity very well.

THIRD WEAKNESS: extreme hostility toward outsiders, confining love to "the brethren." The Fourth Gospel describes the adversaries of Jesus in extremely harsh terms, expecially "the Jews." The devil is their father, a murderer from the beginning; he is a liar and correspondingly they refuse to believe the truth (John 8:43–46,55). They prefer darkness to light because their deeds are evil (3:19–21; 12:35); indeed, God has blinded their eyes (12:40). When the focus of Johannine dispute turned from external non-believers to internal schism, as witnessed in the Epistles, it is noteworthy that this same opprobrium is applied to the secessionists. They are like Cain who belonged to the Evil One and killed his brother (I John 3:12); they are the children of the devil who is a sinner from the beginning (3:8–10). They are liars (2:22) and have a Spirit of Deceit opposed to the Spirit of Truth (4:1–6). The darkness has blinded their eyes (2:11).

Such hostile language is well attested in the inner Jewish disputes of the time.[161] Nevertheless, on the surface it is difficult to reconcile apparent hatred with an observance of *the* commandment of Jesus in the Fourth Gospel: To love one another as I have loved you (John 13:34; 15:12,17). That commandment is exceedingly important to the epistolary author as well, for he places it on the same level as faith in Jesus (I John 3:23). Over and over he insists that it is a commandment of God to love one's brother or one another (I John 2:7–11; 4:21; II John 4–6). I said that *on the surface* hostility toward others is difficult to reconcile with this commandment until we notice that it concerns only loving one another or loving one's brother.[162] There is no demand to love one's neighbor as in the Synoptic tradition (Matt 5:43; Luke 10:27), where the context makes clear that the neighbor includes enemies and strangers (Matt 5:44; Luke 10:29–37). Thus one may say that the Johannine tradition places no emphasis on love of outsiders; John's ideal is a love of God's children who have come into existence through faith in Jesus. If in the Epistles that love does not seem to reach to the secessionists, it is because they have gone out and are no longer community members or children of God. (One may well suspect that the secessionists had the same attitude toward the epistolary author and his adherents.)

In other words, the closeness to Jesus that is the great strength of the ecclesiology of the Fourth Gospel tended to produce an ingroup for whom most others constituted an evil outside world. (I say "most others" because an exception is made for the other sheep who

---

161. Sadducean high priests crucified Pharisees in the time of Alexander Jannaeus. The Qumran Essenes report an attempt by the Jerusalem priesthood to kill their Teacher, and for them the high priest was a Man of Lies.

162. In our language the Johannine commandment would involve loving one's brother and sister; for, as I have stressed (p. 94), women played an important role in Johannine thought.

are not of this fold in John 10:16—a sign that there were non-Johannine Christians who were not considered evil.[163]) In the Gospel "the Jews" are the prime example of the world that refuses to believe in Jesus (John 16:8–9); in the Epistles the secessionists belong to the world (I John 4:5). The famous verse, "God loved the world so much that He gave His only Son" (John 3:16), should not be misunderstood. That giving of the Son, that sending of the light into the world, produces a division between those who come to the light because they act in truth and those who prefer darkness to light because their deeds are evil (3:19–21). Subsequently in the Gospel, the world and darkness are generally equated as constituting the realm of Satan who is the Prince of this world (12:31; 14:30; 16:11). That is why Jesus does not pray for the world (17:9), and his followers, though in the world, are not of it (17:14–18). This attitude carries over to the Epistles where the author speaks of "a sin unto death"— surely the secessionist refusal to believe, exhibited by leaving the community—and observes, "I do not say that one should pray about that" (I John 5:16–17).

On the positive side, love for one's fellow Christian is essential for the survival of the church. In Roman Catholicism after Vatican II there has been great emphasis on the need to show love for all, Christian and non-Christian. At the same time, however, the changes put into effect through Vatican II have led to sharp dispute within the church, so that Catholics who were relatively harmonious before the council are now divided among themselves. There is violent vituperation of moderates and liberals by ultra-conservatives, and contempt for conservatives by liberals, an experience all too common in Protestant churches as well. Small wonder that all our concern for outsiders is not overly convincing as Christian witness since often those outsiders do not see love for one another within our churches. The secular adage that charity or love should begin at home has its wisdom.

---

163. In *Community* 81–88, I suggest that these other sheep were the Christians of the Apostolic Churches, i.e., churches that venerated apostles like Peter and Paul as their founders, churches visible in the NT in the post-Pauline works (Chapters 2 – 4 above), in the Roman church that produced I Peter, and in the church of Matthew. The Johannine attitude toward Jewish Christians who associated themselves with James the brother of the Lord would be more hostile (ftnote 148 above).

On the negative side, too narrow a Christian focus of love, whereby the only real interest is for one's own, does little justice to a Jesus who was truly concerned with outsiders, i.e., the sinners, the tax collectors, and the prostitutes. (Is it accidental that such an outreach is not described at all in the Fourth Gospel? Rather the Last Supper begins with the words, "Having loved *his own* . . . , he loved them to the very end" [13:1].) In the preceding chapter, I mentioned Christian sectarian groups for whom John is *the* gospel because they can interpret it as favoring their theology of Jesus as "my personal savior." It is not surprising to find that generally such groups show little interest in ecumenism or in relations with the larger and more traditional churches. The Fourth Gospel was written by a spokesman for a group persecuted by outsiders, and it will always be more congenial to those whose primary concern is for their own.

At the end of Chapter 3 above, I observed that the concentration on the church in Colossians/Ephesians leaves the non-Christian world out of consideration. At the end of Chapter 5, I observed that the somewhat exclusive "people of God" concept in I Peter gives no attention to holiness among the majority who are not of this people. Yet problems of neglect toward and of silence about the outside world are not nearly so serious as the problem raised by the Johannine writings which, while they never say, "Hate the world," do say, "Have no love for the world" (I John 2:15).[164]

FOURTH WEAKNESS: uncontrollable divisions caused by appeal to the Paraclete. Perhaps the most serious weakness in Johannine ecclesiology and the one most apparent in the Epistles centers on the role of the Paraclete. The thought that there is a living divine teacher in the heart of each believer—a teacher who is the ongoing presence of Jesus, preserving what he taught but interpreting it anew in each generation—is surely one of the greatest contributions made to Christianity by the Fourth Gospel. But the Jesus who sends the Paraclete never tells his followers what is to happen when believers who possess the Paraclete disagree with each other. The Johannine Epistles tell us what frequently happens: they break their *koinōnia* or

---

164. To avoid the problem some commentators would argue for subtly different senses of "world" in the Johannine writings. In *Epistles* 223–24, 323–25, I resist that temptation, for I think we must face up to the limitations of Johannine thought.

communion with each other. If the Spirit is the highest and only authority and if each side appeals to him as support for its position, it is nigh impossible (particularly in a dualistic framework where all is either light or darkness) to make concessions and to work out compromises.

In the divisive situation encountered in the Johannine Epistles the author appeals to tradition as it was "from the beginning" as a partial support for his interpretation. (The secessionists probably appealed to the import of Fourth Gospel formulations.) But it is very clear that he is counting on the fact that his readers have been anointed with the Spirit and so can recognize the truth from him when they hear it. If the author were a presbyter-bishop in the model of the Pastorals, he could silence his adversaries by his own authority (Titus 1:11). One of his tasks as an appointed teacher would have been the discernment of sound doctrine (Titus 2:1). But the author of the Epistles of John is bound by the Johannine tradition that the Paraclete is the one who guides people along the way of truth (John 16:13). Consequently, even in the midst of this great schism, he must write, "The anointing you received . . . abides in you; and so you have no need for anyone to teach you" (I John 2:27).

Noble as it is, his principle did not and will not work. The secessionists who had been members of the Johannine community were anointed with the Paraclete-Spirit, and that anointing which is supposed to be "true and free from any lie" (I John 2:27) did not save them from becoming liars. (Of course, it is the author who judges them to be liars [2:22]; certainly in their judgment he is the liar.) The author is writing I John and II John because he feels that those still in communion with him are endangered by secessionist propaganda. How can there be any danger if they are guided by the Paraclete, the Spirit of Truth? The author faces up to that issue by pointing out that there is a Spirit of Deceit as well as a Spirit of Truth, and that one must test the Spirits (4:1–6). The test he offers is that the people who listen to him (and his fellow tradition-bearers) have the Spirit of Truth, while those who disagree with him have the Spirit of Deceit. One can well imagine that the opposite is being urged by the secessionists: if you agree with us, you have the Spirit of Truth. And in point of fact, the author seems to admit that the secessionists are winning numerically in this tug of war, for "the world listens to them" (4:5).

In my judgment there is no way to control such a division in a Paraclete-guided community of people. The Johannine community discovered that, for it split up and went out of existence. In my *Community*, working from second-century evidence, I suggested that the larger group of Johannine Christians, who were of secessionist persuasion, drifted off into gnosticism, carrying the Fourth Gospel with them. Another group came to terms with the main body of Christians whom Ignatius calls "the church catholic" (*Smyrneans* 8:2)—a church that had teachers such as the presbyter-bishops, and eventually the single bishops of each region. Much to the epistolary author's annoyance, according to III John 9-10, Diotrephes seems already to be taking to himself such a role. The epilogue to the Fourth Gospel, which may represent the final stage of the Johannine writings preserved for us, acknowledges the authority of a human shepherd (John 21:15-17), even if it hedges that authority with Johannine safeguards (p. 93 above). Thus, one branch of the Johannine community had to come to grips with the ecclesiology of the Pastorals, stodgy and formal as it is, in order to become part of a non-gnostic Christianity.

I presume that the reader of this chapter and of the preceding chapter has detected my admiration for the Johannine insights about the relation of Christians to Jesus. Johannine ecclesiology is the most attractive and exciting in the NT. Alas, it is also one of the least stable. One rejoices that at the end of the first century, when much about the church was being formalized and institutionalized, there were Christians who still marched to the sounds of a different drummer; and one is sad that the road down which they went was inevitably a dead end. But their witness lives on in the many-faceted great "church catholic" that brought their Gospel into its canon. Even if that Gospel cannot be the only guide for the church catholic, and even if alongside the Beloved Disciple (and indeed over him) have been placed the apostles, such as Peter and Paul, the community of the Beloved Disciple continues to bear warning witness that the church must never be allowed to replace the unique role of Jesus in the life of Christians.

CHAPTER 8

The Heritage of Jewish/Gentile Christianity in Matthew: Authority That Does Not Stifle Jesus

W E TURN NOW to the ecclesiology of the gospel that the church has placed first in the canon, Matthew. Leaving aside the historical reasons for that ordering,[165] we must acknowledge that Matthew has an unassailable ecclesiological priority. It is the only gospel that uses the word "church." Of all the gospels it was best suited to the manifold needs of the later church, the most cited by the church fathers, the most used in the liturgy, and the most serviceable for catechetical purposes. In critical scholarship of the last two centuries Mark has drawn attention as the oldest gospel; and today often in seminary curricula, if there is going to be only one exegetical gospel course, it will be centered on Mark. But for a millennium and three-quarters Mark was virtually obliterated by Matthew,[166] and Mark had no influence on church life. Luke may be a more serious rival for Matthew in the affection of Christians, but Luke is not really comparable when it comes to basics. People who know by heart the Lucan

---

165. Matthew was thought to have been written by one of the Twelve, written first, written in Hebrew or Aramaic (the language of Jesus), and written as the most complete account. Most of those theories would have no serious following today, although there are some very vocal critical scholars who argue that Matthew anteceded Mark.

166. Some 600 of Mark's 661 verses are reused by Matthew, and so little need was felt to read Mark itself.

form of the Lord's Prayer could probably hold meetings in a tele-phone booth; the number of people who know Matthew's form of the Lord's Prayer is coterminous with the number of Christians in the world. Those who are even aware that Luke has four beatitudes are very few, while Matthew's eight beatitudes have been committed to memory and heart by countless believers. Only students are aware that Luke has a Sermon on the Plain, while even for non-Christians Matthew's Sermon on the Mount is the quintessential message of Je-sus. The evangelist we call Matthew had a genius for collection and organization that made his gospel the best guide to practical Chris-tian life.

Alas, Matthew has been neglected by a critical scholarship too little interested in the service of the church. In the major languages we are still deficient in up-to-date, full-scale critical commentaries on Matthew.[167] Nevertheless, there are signs of a resurgent scholarly in-terest in Matthew, and superb monographs on the theology of Mat-thew have appeared.[168] I recommend two excellent short studies of the purpose and thrust of the gospel: Kingsbury, *Matthew,* and Meier, *Vision.*

For the purposes of detecting life in the last third of the first century (the Sub-Apostolic Period), Matthew is almost as revelatory as John, perhaps because these two gospels are written in strongly adversary situations. Luke wrote a separate Acts of the Apostles to recount what happened to the followers of Jesus after the resurrec-tion, and therefore the Gospel of Luke in itself is not overly indica-tive of church life. For Matthew, however, there is no time of the church separated from the time of Jesus.[169] Both Matthew and John have interwoven their understanding of the post-resurrectional era into the account of Jesus' public ministry[170] (although this two-level technique [p. 104 above] is most consistent in John). In Matthew, for

---

167. The best commentaries available in English are relatively short, e.g., E. Schweizer, *The Good News According to Matthew* (Atlanta: Knox, 1975); J. P. Meier, *Matthew* (New Testament Message 3; Wilmington: Glazier, 1980).

168. See the Select Bibliography in Kingsbury, *Matthew* 110-12.

169. Unlike the Lucan Jesus who goes away by ascending into heaven (Luke 24:51), the Matthean Jesus continues on with his followers until the end of time (Matt 28:20).

170. There is, of course, post-resurrectional insight in Mark; but it is not clear how that includes the history of Christianity known to Mark. See pp. 28–29 above.

instance, those who are presented as hostile are a blend of the adversaries of Jesus' own lifetime and of the adversaries encountered by Matthew's community in post-70 Judaism when the Pharisee rabbinic establishment at Jamnia had become a dominant authority,[171] and when the Sadducee priests, important in the death of Jesus, were fading into history.[172] A firm memory that during his own lifetime Jesus dealt only with Israel and not with Gentiles (Matt 10:5–6) is combined with a gradually gained understanding that the apostolate to which the risen Jesus committed his followers included all nations (28:19). The Twelve are the spokesmen of a misunderstanding of Jesus, downplaying his suffering—a presentation pertinent to Jesus' ministry that Matthew got from Mark—but also spokesmen of a profound faith in Jesus as the Son of God, derived from divine revelation after the resurrection (14:32–33, compared with Mark 6:51–52; Matt 16:15–23, compared with Mark 8:29–33).

Analyzing the blended pre-resurrectional and post-resurrectional picture in Matthew, I would share the majority opinion that the author was a reflective Jewish Christian and a former scribe. The meticulous technique of glossing the infancy narratives and sections of the ministry with OT quotations which are seen as fulfilled (cf. Matt 4:12–17 with Mark 1:14–15) has been interpreted as work done in a school where various versions of the Scriptures would be available.[173] The esteem for a perceptive scribe in 13:52 is probably autobiographical: "Every scribe who has become a disciple of the kingdom of heaven is like a householder who brings out of his treasure what is new and what is old." Matthew's harsh treatment of scribes and Pharisees opposed to Jesus betrays a frustration that in

---

171. Particularly important on Jamnia is W. D. Davies, *The Setting of the Sermon on the Mount* (Cambridge Univ., 1964). Even during Jesus' lifetime it may well have been that the Pharisees were the only group he took seriously enough to argue with—the Sadducees were aristocrats and politicians but seemingly not a real religious force among the people; the Essenes were a sincere but largely withdrawn, quasi-monastic group. By Matthew's time the Pharisees were the only effective "sect of the Jews" left.

172. Whence five references to the Pharisees and Sadducees as if they were a single group (Matt 3:7; 16:1,6,11,12).

173. This insight was made famous by K. Stendahl, *The School of St. Matthew and Its Use of the Old Testament* (Philadelphia: Fortress, 1968) who describes the author as a converted rabbi working with associates. That may need some qualification, but the idea of *studied* application of the OT is valid.

their blindness they cannot see, as the evangelist has seen, that Jesus does not contradict the best of their religious values but really preserves them.[174] "Do not think that I have come to abolish the Law and the Prophets; not to abolish them have I come, but to fulfill them" (5:17). The Pharisees began as a liberalizing movement which, through appeal to oral tradition, sought to make contemporary the real thrust of the written Law of Moses. The problem in Matthew's eyes (and here he may well reflect Jesus) was that this oral interpretation had now become as rigid as the written tradition,[175] and at times was counterproductive. The Jesus who says over and over "You have heard it said, but I say to you" (5:21,27,31,33,38,43) is, then, preserving the purpose of the Law by making certain that a past contemporization of God's will is not treated as if it were exhaustive of that will. The Matthean Jesus is more demanding of people in regard to the Law than the legalists who have set fixed boundaries to what God wants. "Whoever relaxes the least of these commandments and teaches this to others shall be called least in the kingdom of heaven ... And, I tell you, unless your righteousness exceeds that of the scribes and Pharisees, you will never enter the kingdom of heaven" (5:19–20). Jesus can be so demanding because he is not a rabbi among other rabbis,[176] but the one supreme teacher (23:8), and the perfect embodiment of righteousness. He is a lawgiver greater than Moses, for he is the lawgiver of the endtime and the supreme interpreter of God's will.[177] He is the Lord, the Son of God.

Parenthetically, let me pause for a few comments about Mat-

---

174. I have encountered a similar phenomenon in students from a fundamentalist background who have learned to use biblical criticism constructively. They can become very annoyed with other fundamentalists who denounce biblical criticism as destructive of the Word of God, precisely because they know from their own experience that this need not be so.

175. Within a century of Matthew's time the oral tradition of the rabbis would be written down as the Mishnah, and then itself become the subject of an oral commentary, the Gemara, which in another three centuries would be written down, forming the Talmud, which would in turn become the subject of more commentary. For the polemical character of Matthew's evaluation of such tradition, see ftnote 185 below.

176. Mark is seemingly content with having Jesus called rabbi, but in Matthew that title is used only by Judas and those who do not follow Jesus.

177. The interpretation in Matt 5:31–32, concerning the certificate of divorce, goes beyond intensifying the demand of the Law, seemingly to the point of contradicting the Law. Matthew 19:3–9, however, makes it clear that the divorce certificate was a concession made by Moses "because of your hardness of heart," but was not God's

thew and Paul. If John Meier (*Antioch* 39–44) is correct, Matthew
was written in an Antioch where Paul had lost out in his fight for a
Law-free regimen for Gentile Christians (Gal 2:11ff.). The thesis is
that when Peter backed away from Paul's position and yielded to
pressure from the adherents of James, Paul felt too isolated to remain at Antioch and went off to Asia Minor and Greece where he
could maintain his position more successfully. The Gospel of Matthew would represent an intermediary position taken at Antioch con-
ciliating the more reasonable adherents of James and of Paul—the
Law *binds* but only as radically reinterpreted by Jesus. In Chapter 1
above, I pointed out that Paul and Matthew (who may well have had
a similar Pharisee scribal training) might have solved a practical
problem about Christian behavior in the same freeing way, even
though Paul would have come to his answer on the principle that
"Christ is the end of the Law" (Rom 10:4), and Matthew would have
regarded the decision as compatible with the principle that "Not the
smallest letter, nor curlicue of a letter, of the Law will pass away until all is accomplished" (Matt 5:18). It is worth noting that these two
attitudes have been possible among intelligent Christians ever since:
some can stress freedom from law, some can stress law sanely interpreted, without either group approving libertines or legalists. In Roman Catholicism, especially in the United States, canon lawyers,
formerly widely dismissed as legalists, have been in the forefront of
promoting the open attitudes of Vatican II, claiming that they were
doing so in fidelity to the law properly understood! Matthew would
have approved; Paul might have been puzzled even at the existence
of codified Christian canon law. A final fascinating contrast: Matthew (23:9) who supports the continuing value of the Law does not
permit the rabbinical title, "Father," while Paul who denies the enduring force of the Law has no qualms about designating himself as a
unique "father" to the Christian community of Corinth (I Cor 4:15).
Such contrary NT views can challenge respectively both clergy who
put great value on titles (Protestants might need to be reminded that

---

intent "from the beginning." In other words, for the evangelist even the written Law is
a contemporization of the will of God at a particular time and cannot be equated simply with that will. See the discussion by B. L. Martin, "Matthew on Christ and the
Law," *Theological Studies* 44 (1983) 53–70, who does not allow any real abrogation of
the Law by the Matthean Jesus.

the Matthean Jesus would not like "Doctor" either) and fundamentalists who think that calling a clergyman "Father" is the mark of the beast.

Returning now to analyzing the Matthean church situation from the pages of the gospel, we detect an ethnically mixed community. The frequent mention of the scribes and Pharisees, the likelihood that the author had been a scribe, the concentration on how Jesus' ethical teaching can be related to the Law—these and other factors suggest that the Matthean tradition was shaped in Jewish Christianity. Indeed, part of the reason for proposing Antioch as a likely candidate for the locale is the early history of Christian conversions among Greek-speaking Jews there (Meier, *Antioch* 22–23). The openness of Matthean Christianity to Gentiles, however, is also clear in the gospel. The two commands to the disciples, "Go nowhere among the Gentiles" (10:5) and "Go make disciples of all nations" (28:19), probably represent the history of Matthew's community: it came into being through a mission to Jews and then opened to Gentiles.

That pattern of Jews then (unexpectedly) Gentiles was not unusual, according to Acts. On p. 103 above I detected some similarities between John's community and the radical Hellenist Christians of Acts 6–8 who broke away from Temple worship and began aggressively to convert Samaritans and Gentiles. Matthew's community would have been closer to a form of the Hebrew Christianity associated by Acts with the Twelve and particularly with Peter[178]—a Christianity loyal to the Temple and Judaism but learning to its reluctant surprise that the Gentiles could receive Christ and had to be accepted. As for loyalty to Jewish cult, Matthew's community seems to observe the Sabbath (24:20), unlike the Johannine community for whom the Sabbath is an alien feast of the Jews (John 5:1,9). Jerusalem is still "the holy city" for Matthew (27:53), even though its sacred house (the Temple) is forsaken and desolate (23:38). Again that attitude is different from that of the Hellenist Stephen for whom God does not dwell in the Jerusalem "house" (Acts 7:48–49), and differ-

---

178. See ftnote 108 above. For Matthew (16:18) Peter is the apostolic foundation-rock of the church. The Christianity associated with Peter would have been intermediary between that of James and of Paul, but all three would be somewhat "to the right" of Hellenist Christianity.

ent from that of John 4:21 where the time is at hand in which the
Father is no longer worshiped in Jerusalem. The amazement of the
conservative Jewish Christians of Matthew's community at the ad-
vent of Gentile converts may have echoed Jesus' reaction to the Roman centurion at Capernaum, "Not even in Israel have I found such
faith. Many will come from the east and the west and recline at table
with Abraham, Isaac, and Jacob in the kingdom of heaven" (Matt
8:10–11). The massive coming of the Gentiles must have caused
pain[179] because temporally and psychologically it was related to the
fact that Jews were no longer coming in numbers to Jesus. And so
the passage goes on, "Meanwhile the sons of the kingdom [i.e., the
Israelites who should have inherited] will be expelled into outer
darkness" (8:12). The parable of the vineyard rented to tenants who
do not return fruit was borrowed by Matthew from Mark 12:1–11,
but a "punch line" is added (Matt 21:43) that betrays the sad realization to which the Jewish Christian author of the First Gospel has
come. To the chief priests, the elders of the people, and the Pharisees
it is said, "The kingdom of God will be taken away from you and
given to a nation producing fruit."

In God's mysterious providence detectable in the Scriptures, the
kingdom proclaimed by Jesus is more acceptable to the nations than
to the Jews. When Jesus begins his ministry in Galilee rather than
Judea, Matthew (4:12–17) sees the fulfillment of Isa 9:1–2: "Galilee
of the Gentiles—the people who sat in darkness have seen a great
light." When Jesus' healing on the sabbath causes a Pharisee plot to
destroy him so that he has to withdraw from the synagogue (Matt
12:9–21), fulfilled is Isa 41:1–4, "I will put my Spirit upon him, and
he shall proclaim justice to the Gentiles . . . and in his name will the
Gentiles hope." The Jewish Christians of Matthew's community
must learn to live at one with the Gentile Christians without envy.
Indeed, this mixed community is referred to as "the church," for the
significant name by which the Christian following will be known is
foreseen by the Matthean Jesus. It is an OT designation: Deut 23:1
(Septuagint), when describing those who must be kept out of the

179. Certainly the blending of Gentiles and Jews in Matthew's church seems less
peaceful than the idyllic picture of a mixed community in Eph 2:11–19.

community of Israel in order to insure purity, calls that community "the church of the Lord." By using "my church" (16:18) of a mixed group, Matthew indicates his faith that according to Jesus' standards the Gentiles do not mar the purity of the true Israel. Once again Jesus becomes the ultimate interpreter of God's will.

The drama of Jew and Gentile believer is placed on the level of divine revelation in the Matthean infancy narrative. That the child to be born to Mary through the Spirit is Emmanuel, "God with us," is first revealed to Joseph, a just Jew; and he obediently accepts it (1:18–25). He stands for the "just," Law-observant Jewish Christians of Matthew's community who by accepting Jesus made the survival and spread of the good news possible. A second revelation is given to the Gentile magi who come spontaneously to find Jesus; nevertheless, they cannot succeed unless the Jewish Scriptures are interpreted for them (2:1–5). These represent the Gentile converts who have come so willingly to adore Jesus, and learned their Christianity through the interpretation of Scripture in Matthew's community. Alas, however, there is a third group: the Jewish king, the chief priests, and the scribes of the people. They have a revelation in and through the Scriptures which they are capable of interpreting to refer to the Messiah; but instead of coming and adoring as the Gentile magi did, they seek Jesus' life (2:3–5,20). In this latter group Matthew sees the Pharisee rabbis of his time from whom, consequently, all hope of the kingdom is taken away.

Inevitably the hostile judgments of Matthew and his followers about the infidelity of the Pharisees brought a response. Matthew (28:15) knows of anti-resurrection propaganda among Jews, and hints at a charge that Jesus was illegitimate (1:18–19). An expected part of Christian life is calumny and persecution (5:10–11; 10:22), stemming both from the synagogues and Jewish sources (10:17,23) and from the Gentile authorities (10:18; 24:9). The sad result is that some Christians are abandoning Jesus (13:21; 24:10). Internal problems too afflict the Matthean community. Its members seem to have been granted charisms[180] similar to some described in I Cor 12:27–28). There are prophets, wise men, and scribes (23:34), and the

---

180. Helpful here is Schweizer, "Observance" 216–23.

prophets require special care (10:41). Disciples have the power to cast out unclean spirits, heal diseases, and raise the dead (10:8); more than that, there is a miraculous faith that can move mountains (17:20). In times of persecution, in Matthew's experience, the Spirit speaks through Christians (10:19–20). Inevitably amid such charisms there are abuses, for false prophets and evildoing miracle workers get mention (7:22–23; 24:5,11).

Another potential source of conflict lies in the fact emphasized by Kingsbury (*Matthew* 97–98) that there were rich people mixed with the poor in Matthew's community. While Luke writes of small sums of money and copper coins, Matthew's form of the tradition inflates this to large sums and adds gold and silver. There is no hesitancy to underline the fact that Joseph of Arimathea who rendered a service to the dead Jesus was a rich man (27:57). Such a mixture of people gives us a chance to detect the pastoral skill exemplified on the Matthean scene. The Lucan Jesus is harsh on the wealthy, for he specifically curses the rich and those who have their fill, while he blesses those who are poor and hungry (Luke 6:20–25). The wealthy barn builder who seeks to reinvest his profit in capital improvement is a fool; he should have given it to the poor (Luke 12:13–21). Poor Lazarus and the rich man have their status reversed in the afterworld seemingly because the possession of wealth here deserves punishment in Hades, while being poor here deserves bliss with Abraham (Luke 16:19–25). Such harshness is not Matthew's style at all. It is true that delight in riches can choke off the fruitfulness of the word of God (Matt 13:22) and that the rich will find it hard to enter the kingdom (19:23); but with God all things are possible (19:26). There is a chance for the rich, since, if they are not poor in fact, they can be poor *in spirit,* and, if they are not physically hungry, they can hunger and thirst *after justice,* and thus be included under Jesus' beatitude (5:3,6)—a beatitude for which in Matthew there is no corresponding curse against wealth and plenty.

Similar pastoral nuance can be detected in facing the other mixtures mentioned above, as illustrated by the parable of weeds growing among the wheat (13:24–30,36–43). If there are false prophets and misbehaving charismatics, if there are weeds that are sons of the Evil One, should not they be torn out of the church or the kingdom of the Son of Man?[181] But the Matthean Jesus warns that such a purge might damage the good members, and so the situation must be tolerated until there comes a divine judgment. Sects can pride themselves on a purism that drives out all who do not meet an ideal, but a church has to show patience and mercy.

The story of the coin in the fish's mouth (17:24–27) is still another example of Matthean nuance. The issue concerned is the payment of the tax imposed on Jews for the support of the Temple or (if a shift occurred in the reference of the story after the destruction of the Temple) the payment of the poll tax imposed by the Romans on Jews (*fiscus judaicus*). After Peter answers that Jesus does pay the tax, this church authority[182] receives from Jesus himself a more precise instruction to the effect that in fact his followers are free from such tax, but in order not to give offense the tax will be paid. The issue is quite understandable among the Jewish Christians of Matthew's church: are they still Jews so that obligations on Jews bind them? Matthew clarifies the principle but shows a pastoral sense about when the exercise of a principle is not worth a major struggle. (In the language of the later church some issues are *adiaphora*.) Matthew's attitude almost echoes Peter's stance at Antioch implicit in Gal 2:11ff. Paul maintained that the food laws did not oblige the Gentiles; evidently Peter agreed but backed away from the exercise of that freedom when the issue gave signs of leading to a struggle with James and Jerusalem. Paul castigates Peter's behavior as a denial of "the truth of the Gospel" (Gal 2:14). But I wonder whether Paul would have seen the issue so strongly if yielding to pressure from the adherents of James would not have involved his own loss of

---

181. The willingness to designate as the kingdom of the Son of Man a group of such mixed character shows that Matthew could appreciate the dignity and holiness of the whole despite the presence of sinners. There is no purism here; nor is there laxity, for a purification must take place before the kingdom of the Father will be a reality where only the good shine (13:40–43).

182. In the ecumenical book, *Peter in the New Testament,* ed. R. E. Brown *et al.* (New York: Paulist; and Minneapolis: Augsburg, 1973) there was agreement that, in portraying Peter as a spokesman for the disciples in addressing Jesus, Matthew was extending the image of Peter into church life after Peter's death. Thus he becomes a symbol of church authorities having to interpret the will of Jesus as they face new issues. As Donfried, *Word* 128, points out, Matthew's description of Peter actualizes the gospel message for the author's time.

face; he is much more subtle about pastoral concessions in I Cor 8 where his prestige is not on the line. Consequently, I would ask if Peter's position at Antioch was not wiser. In any case, the lesson from the Matthean tax issue is important: an exercise of freedom is, at times, better avoided because of offense—a lesson all the more important when a strong stance that is being advertised as a defense of the Gospel may involve personal prestige.

A final example of Matthean nuance leads us into the whole issue of church authority. Despite what he rejects as Pharisee legalism, we have seen that Matthew refuses to dispense with the Law; rather he argues that Jesus' non-legalism is true to the Law. Although he despises Pharisee posturing and claims of precedence (23:5–7), Matthew does not reject indiscriminately for his community the Pharisee principles of authority. In 23:1–2 the Matthean readers are told, "The scribes and Pharisees sit on the chair of Moses, so practice and observe whatever they tell you; but do not do what they do." Since other passages in the gospel clearly reject what the Pharisees "tell" (e.g., 15:6), some scholars think that Matthew has preserved here a fossil of an earlier obedience when Jews and Jewish Christians still attended the same synagogue.[183] Others would see 23:1–2 as Matthew's gesture toward the more conservative in his Christian community who have not been able to wean themselves away from dependence on the Jewish authorities, but a gesture that retains a criticism of Pharisee practice as not befitting Christians. In any case, the idea of a chair of authoritative judgment is not alien to Matthew's Christianity, for elsewhere we hear that the Twelve who followed Jesus are to sit on twelve thrones judging the tribes of Israel (19:28). Even if that is to take place only "in the new world," rabbinic models of authority are not far from Matthew's mind and seem to be tolerable so long as it is recognized that ultimately the authority comes from Jesus.

---

183. We are uncertain of the exact position of Matthew's community vis-à-vis the local synagogue. Did Jews and Jewish Christians still worship together? Did they each have their own synagogues (see "their synagogues" in 10:17), but not yet think of one another as a different religion? Or does the reference to a local church in 18:17 indicate that the synagogue of the Jews and the church of the Christians had now wholly separated? As I pointed out in reference to the Sabbath, the separation was not as sharp as what is described in John.

Again, Peter and the disciples are given the power to bind and loose, a power clearly phrased in rabbinic terms.[184] Some have proposed that consciously or unconsciously Matthew thinks of Peter as the chief rabbi of the church, although that designation never appears. The imagery of the keys to the kingdom that are given to Peter (16:19) has its roots in Isa 22:22 as an expression for the power of the prime minister in the Davidic kingdom who controls access to the king. Once more all these are instances of power given *by Jesus,* but they lucidly demonstrate that Matthew's church has a strong sense of organization and authority. That very fact explains why Matt 23:8-11 takes pains to forbid the use of rabbinic titles (Rabbi, Father, Master). With so many features of Jewish authority taken over by the Matthean church from the synagogue and/or the Jamnia school as part of the blending of the new with the old, the wise Christian scribe who writes the gospel must take precautions lest the spirit of the Pharisees enter the church.

STRENGTHS AND WEAKNESSES

One must deal with the issue of ecclesiological strengths and weaknesses differently in treating Matthew. In the Pauline and Petrine writings I pointed out the respective ecclesiological strengths by analyzing the works themselves, and then from church experience I called attention to weaknesses inherent in those strengths if they were taken in isolation. In the Johannine writings I pointed out ecclesiological strengths in the way that the Fourth Gospel presents the disciples and Jesus, but from the Epistles of John showed that a schism had developed, exploiting the weaknesses in the community shaped by the Fourth Gospel. What I have written in the first part of this chapter illustrates the two great strengths of Matthew's ecclesiology. *First,* there is inculcated a high respect for the Law and for authority. The sentiments of 9:8 might well describe faithful members of the Matthean community: "They glorified God who had giv-

---

184. This power is referred to in 16:19 and 18:18, but we are not certain that it has the same meaning in both places. It can refer to the power of making decisions in the name of Jesus that bind or loose in conscience the whole church (16:19?) and/or to the power of admitting to or excluding from the (local) community (18:18?).

en such authority to men." *Second,* the evangelist shows a remarkable nuance in dealing with pastoral issues, thereby making certain to preserve the attitudes of Jesus in interpreting the Law and exercising authority. If only the first strength were present in Matthew, this section of my chapter would stress the inherent weakness of a firm morality inculcated through an adherence to law and authority, namely, the dangers of legalism, authoritarianism, and a type of clericalism. But through the evident second strength Matthew already seeks to protect the community against precisely those dangers by insisting that the voice of Jesus must be heard in the church. Matthew's approach is not just "You have heard it said" (which would be equivalent to law) but also "I say to you" (which keeps alive a vibrant demand, preventing past law from absolutizing God's will). Vehicles through which authority is to be exercised are featured (Peter, the disciples, the whole community); but the evangelist insists that they all get their power from Jesus and must exercise it according to his standards. Matthew is aware that, left on their own, the authoritative figures would inevitably begin to act like the scribes and Pharisees; and by the attacks of Jesus on the Jewish authorities Matthew corrects incipient attitudes within the church. The uniqueness of the First Gospel, then, is that, because of an ongoing unhappy confrontation with a Judaism dominated by Pharisees, the author shows an awareness of the weaknesses and dangers inherent in the church's adherence to law and authority[185] and has built in a corrective.

In treating Johannine Christianity I spoke of the importance accorded therein to an ongoing presence of Jesus particularly in and through the Paraclete, the living teacher. Matthew's equally strong sense of the continued presence of Jesus (28:20: "I am with you always to the end of the age") has a different tone. The teaching of Jesus, exemplified in the five great sermons of the First Gospel,[186] is the

---

185. All of this is from Matthew's perspective which was colored by polemics. Jewish scholars rightly point out that many of the rabbis of the period were quite aware of the dangers of legalism and authoritarianism and that they worked against those dangers from within Pharisee Judaism. Alas, polemics always obscure nuance on the other side.

186. The Sermon on the Mount (chaps. 5 – 7), the Sermon on the Mission (10), the Sermon in Parables (13), the Sermon on Church Order and Life (18), the Eschatological Sermon (24 – 25).

means in and through which Jesus remains present to a community that is willing to live by his commandments. This is caught up in the Matthean phrase "the gospel of the kingdom" that introduces the Sermon on the Mount (4:23).[187] For Paul "the gospel" is the good news of what God has done through Jesus, "put to *death* for our trespasses, *raised* for our justification" (Rom 4:25). For Mark (1:1) "the gospel of Jesus Christ" is broader and includes the story of what Jesus did during his ministry, which makes the death and resurrection more intelligible. But Mark is a gospel of deed with only a relatively small body of teaching. By incorporating the Q sayings material, Matthew has changed the proportion so that "the gospel of the kingdom" now consists very heavily in the teaching by which Jesus made God's reign present to people's lives. "Jesus went about all the cities and villages, teaching in their synagogues and preaching the gospel of the kingdom" (Matt 9:35). Therefore, a Christianity shaped by Matthew will not absolutize the gospel even in the church without the component of the teaching of Jesus. I have pointed out above (p. 51) that the tendency to identify church and kingdom was growing at the end of the first century, especially in terms of seeing the church as the kingdom of the Son (of Man). Matthew abets that tendency in the explanation of the parable of the weeds (13:36–43), but his understanding of "the gospel of the kingdom" means that the church-kingdom must be a place where Jesus' teaching is lived. If believing church members are "the sons of the kingdom" (13:38), replacing the Jewish "sons of the kingdom" who did not believe (8:12), they deserve that title only because they live by "the gospel of the kingdom."

Early in this chapter I wrote that Matthew has interwoven his understanding of the post-resurrectional era into the account of Jesus' public ministry, writing, as it were, his Acts of the Apostles in and through the gospel. He thus combines the ongoing church situation with a scenario where the dominant figure is Jesus the ethical teacher, Jesus the righteous interpreter of the Law. (We saw that John also reads the post-resurrectional situation back into the ministry, but into a minstry where there is virtually no ethical teaching!) In Matthew Jesus' commandments bind the disciples (i.e., disciples

---

187. For this insight I am indebted to Schweizer, "Observance" 217–18.

of Jesus' lifetime and disciples at the time of Matthew's gospel) so seriously that only those teachers who *do* the commandments will be considered great in the kingdom of heaven (5:19). All this implies that the one evangelist to use the word "church" and to speak of Jesus' building or founding the church understood the possibility that the church might become a self-sufficient entity, ruling (in the name of Christ, to be sure) by its own authority, its own teaching, and its own commandments. To counteract that danger, Matthew has insisted that the church should rule not only in the name of Jesus but also in the spirit of Jesus, and by *his* teaching and *his* commandments. To the extent to which the church is an institution or a society with law and authority, it will tend to be influenced by sociological principles and conformed to the societies of the surrounding culture—in Matthew's situation, conformed to the synagogue and the Pharisee rabbinical structures. Matthew accepts institution, law, and authority but wants a unique society where the voice of Jesus has not been stifled and remains normative. Only then "will this gospel of the kingdom be proclaimed throughout the whole world as a testimony to the nations" (24:14).

*   *   *

Let me make a final contribution to this NT discussion of the churches the apostles left behind by considering the remarkable chap. 18 of Matthew that has been called Jesus' Sermon on Church Order and Life. This may well be the most profound practical treatment of church in the NT and exemplifies Matthew's nuance in anticipating the dangers that the church faces from the very fact that it is structured and has authority. The sermon is addressed by Jesus to "the disciples," and there is a dispute among scholars whether that means the Twelve or all Christians.[188] What cannot be disputed is

---

188. In Matthew's source (Mark 9:33–37) the Twelve are specifically mentioned. In the Matthean setting Peter has been the subject of the preceding scene where "Jesus spoke to him first" (17:25). It would make sense, then, that the disciples (meaning the other members of the Twelve) ask somewhat jealously about who is the greatest in the kingdom of heaven.

that much of the chapter is directed to those who act with authority in the church and have pastoral responsibility.[189]

The chapter begins with a question posed by the disciples, "Who is the greatest in the kingdom of heaven?" Some would argue that Matthew thinks of "kingdom" purely eschatologically, and so the question is equivalent to "Who is going to be highest in heaven or at the end of time?" However, as we have seen, Matthew tends to localize and reify "kingdom" and identifies the church on earth as the kingdom of the Son of Man. Certainly the rest of the chapter deals with church practice on earth, and so it is not impossible that this question reflects partially on primacy in the church. If so, Matthew shows an excellent instinct about what becomes important in a religious society where there is authority. The very imagery of kingdom raises the issues of prestige and power—issues that Jesus regarded as a temptation of the devil seeking to reduce the kingdom of God to the level of a kingdom of this world (Matt 4:5–10). Envy about primacy will manifest itself whether church authority is exercised through charisms or offices. In the situation of I Cor 12–14 there is clearly a dispute over which charism is best to have. Although Paul tries to quell it by speaking about the importance of love, he always lists apostles first in the charisms; and we remember that he is an *apostle!* In a structure with offices exemplified by the presence of presbyter-bishops in the Pastorals, there was rapid development of the office of the single bishop *over* the presbyters. That development becomes a major point for Ignatius, *ca.* A.D. 110; and we remember that Ignatius is the *sole bishop* of Antioch! In later times both the schism between the East and the West and the inner-Western schism of the Reformation featured prominently a dispute about the primacy of the Bishop of Rome in the whole church. In other

---

189. We do not know whether there were offices (presbyter-bishops, deacons) in the Matthean community or only authoritative charisms. The mention in the gospel of apostles, prophets, wise men, and scribes (see 23:34) has been thought to favor the latter; but do wise men and scribes exhibit charisms? *Pace* Schweizer, "Observance" 228, Matthew's failure to mention presbyters and bishops proves nothing, for that would be the type of blatant anachronism that Matthew avoids in his gospel. "Shepherd" was a set image in the late first century for presbyter-bishops (Acts 20:28; I Peter 5:2–4; perhaps John 21:15–17), and Matt 18:12–14 does speak of the responsibility of shepherds.

words, sociology will not allow an organized society, religious or otherwise, to avoid the issue of who has the greatest authority. In the practical language of business, the first question when one is trying to analyze and deal with a large corporation is, "Who has the 'heft' here?"

By the standards of other societies the greatest authority or power makes one the greatest figure in the group. Matthew would argue that such a norm cannot be allowed in the church where Jesus' standards must override. The answer to the question of who is the greatest in the kingdom (or in the church where the gospel of the kingdom is proclaimed) is given through the example of a little child. This is not because, as romantics would have us think, the little child is thought of as lovable, or cuddly, or innocent, but because the child is helpless and dependent, with no power.[190] In the kingdom of heaven God has supreme power or authority; closeness to God and therefore greatness in the kingdom comes according to the degree in which people surrender themselves to God, putting Him first in their lives. When God rules a person's life, then that person is great in God's kingdom.[191] The value system of the kingdoms of this world is upside down in relation to the kingdom of heaven, for in Jesus' eyes not power but a lack of it can make a person great. The first issue for a church that is going to survive in the world as Jesus' society is how to avoid accepting the upside-down values of the surrounding societies. In his treatment of church life, Matthew has the disciples bring that issue to the fore by their opening question, so that from the beginning of the Sermon the otherness of Jesus' teaching may be clear.

The section that follows in Matt 18 (vv. 5–9) deals with scandal. All disciples, even those in authority, have been invited to have the outlook of children; but the warning against scandalizing "one of these little ones" shows special sensitivity toward the most vulnerable members of the community. The language of this passage is too much a set tradition (see Matt 5:29–30) for us to know whether seri-

---

190. When the disciples are told to humble themselves like little children (18:4), we recall that Jesus himself is humble (11:29). The Messiah and Son of God who has to face death at the disposition of God's will (26:39,42) and to experience dying without assistance (27:46) exemplifies what makes one greatest in the kingdom.

191. In a sense John is dealing with this same issue when he puts more emphasis on the Disciple whom Jesus loved than on Peter (the apostle).

ous scandals had actually occurred in the history of the Matthean community, especially scandals given by those who were supposed to be leading the church. When this has happened in history, those disillusioned by the scandal have sometimes been lost to the church permanently; and so Matthew, by foresight if not by hindsight, has good reason to introduce severe warnings of Jesus about the issue.

More interesting for our purposes is the next section (18:10–14) beginning with a warning not to despise the little ones. The attitudes of church authorities, sometimes even the unconscious attitudes, may be more scandalous than their behavior. What would Matthew have thought about II Tim 3:6–7 with its low estimate of weak women who can never arrive at a knowledge of the truth, especially if that estimate is unconsciously extended so that most of the non-teachers are assumed to be incapable of thinking for themselves (see pp. 42–46 above)?

The section continues with a parabolic lesson about searching for the one stray sheep. Since at this period the shepherd was a frequent symbol for the figure with pastoral responsibility, the issue involves pastoral obligation toward a misled member of the community. Again Matthew shows an appreciation of the likely direction of behavior in an organized society. I spoke earlier of "the Caiaphas principle" based on John 11:49–50: it is better to let one person perish than to have the whole institution destroyed. That is how societies work in this world! Organizations would be delighted with 99% preserved and only 1% lost: that would earn a super-efficiency citation. Any politician who could hold on to 99% of his constituency would have the most favorable poll ratings in history. A lost or strayed one-out-of-a-hundred would be dismissed as better than "par for the course." But Matthew insists that his community must have a different set of values, namely, the values of a Jesus who came to save lost sinners and whose own example as a shepherd must be the model for church shepherds.[192] In fact, however, no large Christian church and scarcely any parish does or can run on the lines of Matthew's parable. The 99% of the members who had not strayed would

---

192. In the similar parable of Luke 15:3–7 Jesus himself is the shepherd seeking out a lost (rather than strayed or misled) sheep which is identified as a sinner. Matthew has adapted the parable to apply more directly to church life.

revolt if they were neglected in favor of the 1% who did stray. They would accuse those in charge of *not being pastoral,* ironic as that may seem. Their plausible argument would be that leaving the ninety-nine in order to search for the one might lead to further losses through neglect, and that therefore it would be better to cut losses by letting the one go.

Yet Matthew cannot be dismissed as parabolic exaggeration. One encounters here an eschatological demand similar to not resisting evil, turning the other cheek when struck, letting someone who takes your coat have the cloak as well (5:39–40), taking nothing along in the task of proclaiming the gospel (10:9–10), selling all that one has to follow Jesus (19:21), paying the one-hour worker as much as the fully employed (20:1–15). No society can run long in this world on such principles, and most individuals cannot put them into practice consistently. Yet they exemplify God's attitudes; and when they are put into practice, at that moment and in that place God's kingdom has been made a reality. If they are ever put into practice universally, "this gospel of the kingdom will have been preached throughout the whole world as a witness to all nations; and then the end will come" (24:14). Therefore, Christians must keep trying to take these eschatological demands seriously, even if in practice only at times are they able to live up to them. The church that every so often, in its care of the ninety-nine, does not stop to worry about the one is not a church attuned to the values of Jesus.

Dealing with the straying or sinful one[193] is also the theme of the following section (18:15–18). While echoing existing disciplinary practice,[194] the section illustrates Matthew's preference that love and not authority should be primary in dealing with a fellow Christian. Once more Matthew shows his keen insight about how most societies work, whether secular or religious. The tendency is not to go directly to the one who is causing a problem but to go over the person's head to someone who has the authority to correct. This avoids confrontation and is more efficient. In the Roman Catholic church, when peo-

---

193. The phrase "against you" in 18:15 ("if your brother sins against you") is probably not original but introduced under the influence of Luke 17:4. Thus the range of the sin is broad.

194. A threefold stage of correction is found in the Qumran Dead Sea Scrolls (1QS 5:25 – 6:1; CD 9:2). The principles come from Lev 19:17–18 and Deut 19:15.

ple do not like what another parishioner is doing, they report it to
the pastor. When they do not like what the pastor is doing, they report it to the bishop. When they do not like what the bishop is doing,
they report it to Rome. All of this is said to be done for the person's
own good and for the purity of religion; but the way Jesus behaved
does not enter the picture. In verse 18 Matthew shows keen awareness that there is authority in the church; but in itself such authority
is neither Christian nor unChristian. That quality comes not only
from the way authority is exercised but also from a reluctance to appeal to it.

Although vv. 19–20 were originally independent, by placing
them where he has, Matthew explains why the whole church community is the court of final resort that can take the action of quaran-
tining or excommunicating the recalcitrant sinner.[195] The community
members gather in prayer in Jesus' name because the issue is clearly
religious and not merely administrative; and in this gathering the ongoing presence of Jesus is activated (28:20; 18:20). The authority to
bind and loose is not to be exercised independently of the Jesus to
whom all authority in heaven and on earth has been given (28:18).
Bureaucratic procedures are inevitable sociological developments,
but Matthew's outlook does nothing to encourage them.

When the recalcitrant "brother" is quarantined or expelled in v.
17, the decision is "Let him be to you as a Gentile and a tax collector"—a judicial sentence reflecting Jewish roots where Gentiles are
outsiders to be consorted with as little as possible, and tax collectors
are public sinners outside the Law. Most commentators assume that
Matthew has taken over the sentence simply as traditional language
so that the former brother is to be shunned. However, must not one
ask what this would mean in a mixed Jewish/Gentile church of the

---

195. Scholars disagree on which of those two actions is meant. Some commentators assume that the community has the authority to take action because there are no
officers in the Matthean church (see ftnote 189 above). Since "binding and loosing"
was entrusted to Peter in 16:19, some Protestant scholars would contend that by Matthew's time the community had replaced Peter. Others would contend that in Matthew's church power was invested both in authorities of whom Peter is a symbol and
in the community acting in unison. Personally I judge it unlikely that the power of the
keys given only to Peter (16:19) is totally expressed in the power of binding and loosing exercised by the community. The power of the keys echoes the role of the prime
minister in the Davidic kingdom (p. 135 above) and seems to suppose exercise by a
person within the community.

80s where the written gospel of the kingdom has a final instruction by Jesus to go out to the Gentiles and teach them (28:19), and wherein Jesus has shown particular interest in a tax collector named Matthew, inviting him to follow (9:9; 10:3)?[196] In other words is the officially repudiated Christian now to be shunned totally, or is he to be the subject of outreach and concern in imitation of a Jesus who was so interested in searching out tax collectors that he was accused of being their friend (11:19)? The latter interpretation would mean that the community is far from finished with brothers or sisters against whom it has had to invoke authority.

The plausibility of the latter interpretation is enhanced by the next section (18:21–22) concerning the ongoing forgiveness of the brother who sins (the same expression used for the object of the corrective procedure in 18:15). Peter is again a figure of authority getting instruction from Jesus on how he should act (p. 133 above). It has been observed that by asking whether seven times would cover the obligation of forgiveness Peter is being legalistic, resembling the lawyer of Luke 10:25–29 who wanted a definition of the neighbor whom he was obliged to love. To the contrary, I have been struck by the generosity of the Petrine "legalism," for to forgive someone seven times would go beyond normal charity. We who think of ourselves as observant Christians are willing to forgive anyone once. If a person offends us in the same way a second time, that begins to be annoying; but we try to be understanding. Perhaps the person did not reflect or really understand when the offense was pointed out and forgiven the first time. But most of us work by baseball rules—three strikes and you are out! Peter is quite noble in extending the rules to seven strikes.

To his gracious proposal is given the incredible answer of Jesus: seventy times seven or an infinite number of times![197] Does not the answer imply that forgiveness must pursue relentlessly the repudiat-

---

196. Elsewhere "many tax collectors" recline at table with Jesus (9:10); and Jesus affirms that tax collectors will enter the kingdom of God before the chief priests and scribes, for they were prompt to believe in the message of John the Baptist (21:31–32).

197. The Greek text leaves us uncertain: 70×7 ($= 490$) times or 77 times; but the import is the same. Clearly Jesus is revising the thrust of Gen 4:24 where the vengeance for Cain was seven times, but the vengeance for Lamech seventy-seven times. Love is now stronger than hate.

ed brother of 18:17 (and not simply wait for his repentance)? Jesus' insistence on forgiveness is exemplified by a striking parable about a servant who received a totally gracious forgiveness of an immense debt, only to refuse forgiveness of a minor debt to a fellow servant.[198] Many times when I have heard chap. 18 of Matthew cited, attention was concentrated on the binding and loosing power to excommunicate. Both before and after in the chapter, Matthew has hedged that power by indications that care for one's brother or sister is more important. His goal is not to protect or emphasize the authority but to prevent its misuse. Matthew, then, is quite different from the Pastorals which are trying to support the exercise of church authority. Evidently Matthew had lived long enough with that authority to know its dangers. Experience teaches that organized societies are more likely to abuse authority than to abdicate it. The order in chap. 18 proclaims that the power to forgive indefinitely is a greater Christian possession than the power to excommunicate. Lest it be accused of laxness, the church is often very careful about forgiving. Yet, the number of people who have turned away from the church because they found it too forgiving is infinitesimal; the number who have turned away because they found it unforgiving is legion. For this reason, Matthew's pastoral judgment on those in the church who refuse forgiveness is the very harsh conclusion of the parable. In their case the Matthean Jesus has defined the unforgivable sin: it is to be unforgiving.

To survive in the world after the death of the apostles the church has had to be a society existing among other societies. A church that lives and acts according to the spirit of Matt 18 will be a society that is distinct from others, one where what counts for wisdom in other societies has not been able to stifle the voice of Jesus who came to challenge much of the religious wisdom of his time. The great anomaly of Christianity is that only through institution can the message of a non-institutional Jesus be preserved. Matthew does much to insure that in the preservation the message will be kept alive and not merely memorialized.

---

198. The annual income of King Herod was 900 talents; thus the 10,000 talents forgiven by the master can be expressed in our terms by "billions." It would amount to about fifty million denarii, contrasted to the hundred denarii not forgiven to the fellow servant.

CONCLUSION

IN THIS BOOK I have *not* dealt with different models of the church given in the NT because no one of the biblical authors discussed intended to offer an overall picture of what the church should be.[199] Had an author wanted to present a model, we may be sure that a more complete and nuanced ecclesiology would have emerged in the respective writing. My goal was more modest and better adapted to the literature studied. I approached a number of NT books looking for an answer, explicit or implicit, to a specific problem, namely: What were Christians in the Sub-Apostolic Period (the last one-third of the first century) being told that would enable their respective churches to survive the passing of the authoritative apostolic generation? There was no evidence in these works that a consistent or uniform ecclesiology had emerged. Rather, writings addressed to different NT communities had quite diverse emphases.[200] Even though each emphasis could be effective in the particular circumstances of the writing, each had glaring shortcomings that would

---

199. The Pastoral Epistles and Matt 18 come closest to doing that, but only as a response to particular problems.

200. These emphases may be contrary and logically in tension with each other, but they are not contradictory; and there is no evidence that any community we studied was excluding (as distinct from correcting) the emphasis in the tradition of another community. It may be worth repeating that we do not know whether Christians in an individual church of this period knew much specific about the NT works associated with other churches, although they may have known about other Christian traditions and styles of life. The great apostles (Peter, Paul, James) were in contact with each other, but we are uncertain whether their disciples of the next generation were in frequent contact with each other.

constitute a danger were that emphasis isolated and deemed to be sufficient for all times. Taken collectively, however, these emphases constitute a remarkable lesson about early idealism in regard to Christian community life.

Living in churches in the twentieth century, what may we conclude from such a study? There are Christians, of course, who still reject the existence of NT diversities. Some do so from a rigid theory of divine inspiration which discounts the human situation of the NT writings and insists that their message must be uniform because only God's voice can be heard. Others reject diversity in the NT because they project on the first century an ideal situation wherein Jesus had planned out the church, the apostles were of one mind in carrying out his directives, and the only ones who differed were the troublemakers condemned by the NT authors. Like most scholars, Roman Catholic and Protestant, I think neither of these ultraconservative objections to NT diversities is tenable from the evidence. I would go farther: religiously, neither is a particularly good solution, and indeed both have been harmful in developing a mature Christian stance capable of recognizing nuance.

On the other hand, some Christian scholars harden the detectable diversity of the NT into dialectic struggles and contradictory stances. No one can show that any of the churches I have studied had broken *koinōnia* or communion with another. Nor is it likely that the NT churches of this Sub-Apostolic Period had no sense of *koinōnia* among Christians and were self-contained conventicles going their own way. Paul is eloquent on the importance of *koinōnia,* and in the Pauline heritage concern for Christian unity is visible in Luke/Acts and in Ephesians. Peter is a bridge figure in the NT, and the concept of the people of God in I Peter requires a collective understanding of Christianity. For all its individualism, the Fourth Gospel knows of other sheep not of that fold and of Jesus' wish that they be one. Matthew has a concept of *the* church and expands the horizons of Christianity to all nations. Most of the NT was written before the major breaks in *koinōnia* detectable in the second century,[201] and so NT diversity cannot be used to justify Christian division

---

201. At the beginning of the Christian movement there was not a fixed body of doctrine but a belief in Jesus that needed articulation. Consequently the NT period involved growing perceptions and formulations about Jesus and about the community

today. We modern Christians have broken *koinōnia* with each other; for, explicitly or implicitly, we have excommunicated each other and/or stated that other churches are disloyal to the will of Christ in major issues. Such a divided situation does not have NT approbation.

If we can neither ignore NT ecclesiological differences nor use them to justify the present *status quo,* how do those differences serve us? Briefly I would say that they strengthen us and they challenge us. First, *they strengthen us.* Most of us belong to a particular Christian church, Presbyterian, Lutheran, Roman Catholic, Methodist, Episcopalian, etc., because we were born into families who were members of that church. Yet as we matured, if we remained loyal to the church of our birth, it was because we found therein features that brought us close to Christ and the love of God. Those who left one church and went to another did so, in part at least, to find what seemed to them a better context for living out the Gospel. Thus church adherence has become a matter of conviction. A study of the diverse emphases in NT churches may illustrate for us the strengths that we admire in our own church and increase our appreciation for how that church has remained faithful to the biblical heritage. For instance, the Sprunt Lectures were given shortly after Rome had declared that Hans Küng could no longer be identified at his university as an accredited professor of Roman Catholic theology. Many attending the lectures asked me privately whether my church was about to undergo another period of heresy purges and were all ecumenical advances to stop. I thought the answer to both questions was no. But the queries enabled me to point out that in its history the

---

that preserved his name—a growth to which the major figures of the first generation made decisive contributions. Of course, there were times when Peter, Paul, and James differed among themselves; but those differences did not cause a break of *koinōnia,* so far as anyone can prove. By the end of the first century, however, some Christian groups were resisting vehemently developments that had taken place in other groups, and the different views held about important issues were becoming truly contradictory. It is then, in my view, that major breakings of *koinōnia* occurred, for instance, in the Johannine community, as attested by I John 2:19. The second century saw a struggle to determine which of the contradictory views best preserved the apostolic understanding and which ones distorted it in a major way. That was the issue of orthodoxy and heresy. It is a travesty to claim that this view means that orthodoxy did not exist until the late second century. The heritage that was finally acknowledged as orthodox existed from the time of Jesus, not in a static but in a developing way.

Roman Church has continued the serious concern for sound doctrine inculcated in the Pastoral Epistles, which has a concomitant instruction to silence those who are upsetting the church (Titus 1:10–11). Abuse of such a concern is always possible and has certainly occurred in Roman Catholic history; but we would make a bad mistake not to recognize that a strong insistence on sound doctrine is both a NT idea and a strength in the Christian picture, often best understood from within.[202]

A use of the NT to strengthen people's appreciation of their own church, however, is scarcely new on the Christian scene. In a divided Christianity we have had a long history of using the Scriptures to prove ourselves right, whether as churches or as individuals. The greater contribution of modern NT studies, therefore, may consist in highlighting the ways in which Scripture can *challenge constructively*. A recognition of the range of NT ecclesiological diversity makes the claim of any church to be absolutely faithful to the Scriptures much more complex. We are faithful but in our own specific way; and both ecumenics and biblical studies should make us aware that there are other ways of being faithful to which we do not do justice. It is a strength for a church like my own to preserve the emphasis on sound teaching authority in the Pastorals; but then such a church may need to examine itself about the role that John gives to the Paraclete-Spirit as a teacher dwelling in each Christian. Conventicle churches that combine Johannine imagery and Pauline charisms may need to examine themselves about the sense of historical continuity that runs from Acts to "the church catholic" of the second century and to ask how their highly individualist stance does justice to that. The governance in every church needs to challenged by the voice of Jesus in Matt 18.

In short, a frank study of NT ecclesiologies should convince every Christian community that it is neglecting part of the NT witness. I do not mean that all churches can or should give the same importance to each NT witness, for our respective histories have oriented

---

202. One of the reasons I am happy as a Roman Catholic theologian is that I prefer the church to take doctrine seriously, even if sometimes it restricts freedom. I would not be happy in a church that allows absolute freedom to theologians because doctrine is not a determinative or living factor in church life. See my critique of part of the contemporary Protestant situation in *Critical Meaning* 121–22.

us (probably irrevocably) to different proportions in our evaluation of the Scriptures. But if churches have accepted the canon of the Bible, they cannot allow their preferences to silence any biblical voice. In the polemics of church division we have virtually done that, because we have often seriously neglected a scriptural witness that lent support to a rival church. I contend that in a divided Christianity, instead of reading the Bible to assure ourselves that we are right, we would do better to read it to discover where we have not been listening. As we Christians of different churches try to give hearing to the previously muffled voices, our views of the church will grow larger; and we will come closer to sharing common views. Then the Bible would be doing for us what Jesus did in his time, namely, convincing those who have ears to hear that all is not right, for God is asking of them more than they thought. That could be the *metanoia* that would prepare the church for the kingdom.

BIBLIOGRAPHY

(See ftnote 1 above for the selective character of the works cited in this volume.)

Barrett, C. K., "Acts and the Pauline Corpus," *Expository Times* 88 (1966–67) 2–5.

———"Pauline Controversies in the Post-Pauline Period," *New Testament Studies* 20 (1973–74) 229–45.

Brown, R. E., and J. P. Meier, *Antioch and Rome* (New York: Paulist/London: Geoffrey Chapman, 1983).

Brown, R. E., *The Community of the Beloved Disciple* (New York: Paulist/London: Geoffrey Chapman, 1979).

———*The Critical Meaning of the Bible* (New York: Paulist, 1981; London: Geoffrey Chapman, 1982).

———*The Epistles of John* (Anchor Bible 30; Garden City, NY: Doubleday, 1982; London: Geoffrey Chapman, 1983).

———*The Gospel according to John* (Anchor Bible 29, 29A; Garden City, NY: Doubleday, 1966, 1970; London: Geoffrey Chapman, 1971).

Bruce, F. F., *Peter, Stephen, James, and John: Studies in Early Non-Pauline Christianity* (Grand Rapids: Eerdmans, 1979); *Men and Movements in the Primitive Church* (Exeter: Paternoster, 1979).

Conzelmann, H., "Die Schule des Paulus," in *Theologia Crucis—Signum Crucis,* ed. C. Andresen and G. Klein (E. Dinkler Festschrift; Tübingen: Mohr, 1979) 85–96.

de Boer, M. C., "Images of Paul in the Post-Apostolic Period," *Catholic Biblical Quarterly* 42 (1980) 359–80.

Donfried, K. P., *The Dynamic Word* (San Francisco: Harper & Row, 1981).

Goppelt, L., *Apostolic and Post-Apostolic Times* (London: Black, 1970; Grand Rapids: Baker, 1977).

Harrington, D. J., *God's People in Christ: New Testament Perspectives on the Church and Judaism* (Philadelphia: Fortress, 1980).

——*Light of All Nations: Essays on the Church in New Testament Research* (Wilmington: Glazier, 1982).

Kertelge, K., ed., *Paulus in den neutestamentlichen Spätschriften* (Freiburg: Herder, 1981).

Kingsbury, J. D., *Matthew* (Philadelphia: Fortress, 1977).

Lake, K., *Landmarks in the History of Early Christianity* (London, Macmillan, 1920; New York: Macmillan, 1922).

LaVerdiere, E. A., and W. G. Thompson, "New Testament Communities in Transition: A Study of Matthew and Luke," *Theological Studies* 37 (1976) 567–97.

Meeks, W., *The First Urban Christians* (New Haven: Yale, 1983).

Meier, J. P., and R. E. Brown, *Antioch and Rome* (New York: Paulist/London, Geoffrey Chapman, 1983).

Meier, J. P., *The Vision of Matthew* (Theological Inquiries; New York: Paulist, 1979).

Schweizer, E., "Observance of the Law and Charismatic Activity in Matthew," *New Testament Studies* 16 (1969–70) 213–30.

Theissen, G., *Sociology of Early Palestinian Christianity* (Philadelphia: Fortress, 1978); *The First Followers of Jesus: A Sociological Analysis of the Earliest Christianity* (London: SCM, 1978).

INDEX OF AUTHORS

This is an index of the pages on which bibliographical information about an author's work appears (in the pattern explained in ftnote 1 above).

INDEX OF SUBJECTS

BOOKS BY RAYMOND E. BROWN (1984)

Paulist Press
New Testament Essays
Priest and Bishop
The Virginal Conception and Bodily Resurrection of Jesus
Peter in the New Testament (editor)
Biblical Reflections on Crises Facing the Church
Mary in the New Testament (editor)
The Community of the Beloved Disciple
The Critical Meaning of the Bible
Antioch and Rome (with J. P. Meier)
The Churches the Apostles Left Behind

Doubleday
The Gospel According to John (2 vols., Anchor Bible Commentary)
The Birth of the Messiah
The Epistles of John (Anchor Bible Commentary)

Liturgical Press (Collegeville, Minn.)
The Gospel and Epistles of John (3rd ed.; NT Reading Guide 13)
The Book of Deuteronomy (OT Reading Guide)
An Adult Christ at Christmas

Prentice Hall
The Jerome Biblical Commentary (editor)

Macmillan
Jesus God and Man

Michael Glazier (Wilmington, Del)
Recent Discoveries and the Biblical World

Many of the above have been published in England by Geoffrey Chapman